Adva

NOT AFRAID T(

James' writing takes the reader on a ride from the backseat of the family sedan and the early days in Moberly, MO., to his long sought out adventure and new life in California. At times, that road was smooth and fairly typical, while with others, it became rocky and turbulent shaping the man he is today. Reading James' book was like looking through a window into his soul, as he passionately captured his life's ups and downs that molded and created who he is now, a man of conviction, compassion, and the desire to make life better for those around him. James' writing style is like sitting down with an old friend for a chat over coffee, including a stroll down memory lane that at times, leaves you amused and laughing, while at others, tearful and sharing in his sadness of a particularly difficult and dark period in his life. This ride with James is testimony of no matter how bumpy the road's twists and turns may be, strong perseverance and a caring heart continues to win on this incredible adventure we call life. As cathartic as I believe this book has been for the author, I also see it as a road map, helpful to others, needing encouragement with their own personal journey. —*Gary Kendall*

• • •

I find Jim's story to be engaging and has so many family dynamics that there is something in this for a diversity of people reading it. He is able to capture so many detailed memories and emotions from his growing up years and certainly the impact of how this history shapes the person he has become. It feels like he is allowing us to read his diary. It is very personal and he gives us a front row seat to observe the nuanced and not-so-nuanced relationship that Jim had with his mother and with his father... I wish I could remember the details of my past as he has done. It probably is a way of making peace with and understanding of one's life experiences. —*San Diego State University Dean Emeritus Joyce Gattas*

• • •

The title of this book says it all. In his memoir, *Not Afraid to Tell You Who I Am*, the author, Jim Rostello, shares the stories of his life with blatant honesty. Many of his stories are laugh out loud hysterical, many are grab a tissue tear jerkers. I was engrossed in this memoir from the first chapter. The relationships chronicled in this book are many, they are varied, and they are moving. Jim Rostello openly shares the complicated father-son relationship he had as a child as he internally struggled to love himself as a closeted gay youth in a rural environment where acceptance of those feelings was unheard of at the time. The author takes you on a journey from his childhood all the way through his adult life describing his family, his Catholic upbringing, his teaching career, and his pursuit to find love and happiness in often risky and unconventional places.

After retirement, the author fulfills a lifelong dream and moves to California. In the chapters following the author's retirement to California to enjoy a life well-earned, he is given an HIV diagnosis. His processing of this HIV diagnosis is emotional and powerful. This book is a must read for anyone who appreciates memoirs and the willingness of the author to expose their truth. As you will read, this author transformed years of beliefs of negative self-worth into gifts of self-affirmation, as well as abundant charitable gifts to enable others to excel in disciplines close to his heart. The discovery that beauty and inner peace, indeed, do come from within was a beautiful turning point in the life of the author. If you or someone you know struggles with low self-esteem, an HIV diagnosis or other serious medical issues, or a longing for happiness, I highly recommend reading this memoir. This could be the shot in the arm for which you have been searching.   —*Dawn Wilson*

• • •

I was amazed at Mr. Rostello's ability to vividly remember the details and emotions of his many experiences. He was able to share his life experiences with readers and provide the detail that brought his memories to life. I was surprised to see that Jim grappled with many of the family dynamics and issues of growing up that I thought only I experienced. I was also inspired to read about how he handled these experiences, and he found the strength to carry on with his life. I found the book to be captivating and could not wait to finish reading it. I am certain that other readers will be pleased to be able to read his work as well.   —*Mary Darling*

NOT AFRAID TO TELL YOU
WHO I AM

NOT AFRAID TO TELL YOU

Who I Am

JAMES ROSTELLO

DOGLOVE
PRODUCTIONS
San Diego, CA

CONTENTS

NOT AFRAID
TO TELL
YOU
Who I Am

IT'S STILL LOVE

THE LOVES IN MY LIFE

Love new as falling snow
   is still love
Kindled by friendship and time
   is love growing
Sometimes brief as Indian Summer
   it's still love
Can be smothered by poisonous passion
   it's still love

Love discovered with only a passing glance
   is still love
Unreachable as the smallest star
   is love
More turbulent than a summer storm
   it's still love

Love forbidden or never meant to be
   is still love
Given by only one
   is love
Shrouded in fear or tragically turned to hate
   it's still love

Some just can't give
   Others won't believe
Too many not able to receive
   it will always be there

It's still Love.

FROM THE AUTHOR

I am a first and one-time author with a special purpose: self-understanding and personal growth through my memoirs. My love of writing came late in life when happiness left me, and depression ruled my days. Putting my memoirs on paper emerged from a writer's group that opened the door to hidden dynamics and the ability to accept my life for whatever it has been.

Teaching geography and psychology for 30 years; traveling the world during a more innocent and different time; designing homes; and real estate endeavors were my passions. My goal for writing is not to make money or become a known author, but giving others a road to happiness and peace.

A love in my life, once said to me: "Jim, you are not hung-up on money, but you like acquiring it." He was right. Financial security has allowed me to give the most meaningful awards and accolades in life; the ones we give to others.

Dog therapy programs, college scholarships, growing the importance of geography and psychology, and encouraging memoir writing are all in my heart.

Come along with me as I spill my heart, soul, and guts in hopes that you will see that your existence belongs only to you and no one else. Most important: You are okay and so are others! Think about your path in life as you read about my journey. Relive the good and bad memories of your personal story. Rethink the myriad of significant others in your life. Let the past empower you, not hold you back.

Note: In my journey with my father, I recall the most important moments in certain parts of my memoirs by including his Italian accent that made him who he was.

CHAPTER 1

ATYPICAL BEGINNINGS

I came into this world in Moberly, Missouri on July 6, 1949.
I was in my early 40s when my mother passed away in 1992, exactly 20 years after my father had passed. Returning home to Moberly, Missouri, to clean out the house so it could be sold took me back to all the years of good and bad memories.

A staircase enclosed in a closet led to an unfinished attic space that my father had never gotten around to finishing so that my brother, Albert, and I could have had separate bedrooms. Incomplete walls and unframed windows were tucked into steep gables on either side of the attic. Cobwebs dangled from the semi-dark eaves where the roof met the open rafters of the upstairs floor joists. Sheets of plywood, which kept me from falling through to the rooms below, delineated paths to boxes of our family history. Searching through the large boxes, I found one of my baby pictures. We had not been the typical all-American family with portraits sitting on a piano in the living room. I couldn't believe a professional portrait of me as a baby existed. I had never seen it.

Damn, you were kinda cute except for those big ears, I thought.

I sat down on the bare floor, legs crossed, holding the picture in my lap. I looked at myself in soft yellow baby clothes. As I ran my fingers around the edge of the beautiful ornate gold frame, I began to cry. *How could so much have gone wrong with such an innocent start in life? Was I happy then? Not normal then, too? God, things could have been so different!* Now I keep that picture on a bookshelf and look at it often, wishing that my life had been better.

My mother always said that World War II had been good for the country in that it finally ended the lagging Depression, though no one she knew wanted us meddling in Europe's mounting tensions. The attack on Pearl Harbor changed all of that. The United States had emerged as the strongest nation in the world even though the war had left its scar on American attitudes. While most Americans were only second or third generation themselves, many citizens at that time thought of immigrants as foreigners.

My mother was first-generation Italian-American, and my father had emigrated from Italy in his 20s. Because of their backgrounds and limited experiences, my parents always talked about the importance of school, and praised and defended teachers.

One day during lunch in the Catholic elementary school cafeteria, I accidentally knocked my milk over onto the canned spinach on my tray. All the students tried to figure out how they could get rid of the spinach rather than eat it. I proclaimed to God that was not my intention, but Sister Bernard made me sit on the floor next to the waste cans in the middle of the lunchroom and eat the milk-logged spinach.

When I got home from school, Mom quickly coaxed out the reason I didn't want to return the next day. Without much consolation, Mom noted, "Jimmie Joe, sometimes teachers, like all people, have bad days. Though you may not have intentionally spilled your milk, this won't be the only time in your life that you'll be blamed for something that isn't your fault. Think of all the good Sister does for you, and just be a man about it. Now grab a brownie and go out and play."

I noticed my mom going toward the phone as I headed outside, so I didn't shut the door all the way and listened as she called Sister Bernard.

"Sister Bernard, I understand Jim spilled his milk in the

spinach today. Whether or not he did this on purpose, I would prefer that you don't embarrass him by disciplining him in front of the entire lunchroom. He is very sensitive and doesn't want to go back to school. I do want to also thank you for all that you do for my two children."

My parents always demanded that my older brother Albert and I earn Cs or higher, which was not always easy at our school. In the sixth grade, I was promised a guitar if I got at least half As and Bs on my grade card. Sloppily, I changed a B to an A to get the right mix. My mother commented that Sister had messed up my card when she corrected my grade. Mom was testing me to see if I would admit what I had done.

"Well, what's done is done, and she doesn't want you to complain about it," I quickly responded; hastily attempting to hide my dishonesty. Needless to say, it was all downhill from there, and I found out just how much my parents despised liars and cheaters.

At supper one evening, my father commented that he had seen Artie from across the street skipping school and doing nothing day after day. My brother sarcastically chimed in, "That's probably why they spell repair: R-E-P-I-A-R on their shop sign."

Dad suggested to Mom that he could drop Artie off at the public high school while he took my brother and me to St. Pius. I never knew what my father said or did to get Artie to go to school with us. He waited outside our house every morning, regardless of the weather, to get into our car. Riding with my brother and me also seemed to motivate him. Two years later, he graduated from high school and proudly presented my father with a beautiful wooden side table he had made in shop class.

One cold, icy winter morning as all of us approached the stop sign in front of the public school, Artie positioned himself, as he always did, to jump out of the car at the crossing as quickly as possible so as not to hold my father up. A girl began to fall on the slick pavement just as she crossed the street, and my father screamed in his heavy Italian accent, "Lookie there at thatta girl. She justa dropped down!" Although Artie didn't say anything, I saw his body tense as he suppressed a giggle. I knew he had picked up on my father's English mistake.

Oh my God. This is big trouble now. Within two days, everyone was asking me if I had dropped down lately and calling my dad a foreigner. After a couple days of heckling, I had had enough. As usual, Mom and Dad were babbling in Italian at the supper table, and I decided to speak up.

"Can't we speak English while we eat?" I asked.

My brother immediately stopped snarfing down his food, leaned back in his chair, and looked at everyone in stark apprehension.

Trying to prevent what I knew was about to happen, I proposed, "It might help you, Dad, to speak better."

My father perked up like a little bird dog finding a covey of quail. "Jesus Christ, dammit to Hell. You are notta proud of me?" He shouted, "I know why. You thinka I'm not as smart as you or can do whatta you can. You're ashamed ofa me. I know you and your brother were laughing atta me the other day when I said thatta girl dropped."

"It's fell, Dad. She fell," I quickly blurted out.

"So, you don't thinka I say things right? You thinka it's easy to come to a new country anda not know howa to talk? Let me tella you some things." He stood up with his hands on the table and told his accent-laden story. "One day, when I had only been in New York for a couple of months, I was walking down the streets. I already had a welding job on a building and money in my pockets. This guy kept following and pointing at me and talking to me. I thought he wanted some money, so I gave him a quarter to buy breakfast and a cup of coffee. He kept on following me. When I went to cross the street, I threw my cigarette butt on the ground. He started yelling and hollering at me as he stomped away. Then it came to me; he wanted to finish my cigarette. He wanted the rest of my cigarette, and I threw it away. If I could find that guy today, I would buy him a hundred cigarettes. Why do you think I spent all those nights listening to you when you were learning to read? Don't you think I want to be able to talk like you?"

My father then began to speak in Italian to my mom. He often did this when he couldn't explain something in English.

Mom straightened her housedress under her as she pulled her kitchen chair close to me and sat down. "Your dad wants me to explain something to you."

I looked straight down at my piece of pie, playing with the meringue using my fork. *It's not as stiff as usual tonight.*

"Your grandparents left your dad and uncle with his aunt in Italy to come here and work the coal mines," my mother began to explain as she scooted the pie away and put her hand on mine. "When they had saved enough money, they sent the fare to Italy to bring your father to America. Your uncle was not allowed to come here because the immigration quota had already been met, and there was a lengthy waiting list. Immigration quota means that no more immigrants were allowed after a certain number. Your father, though only getting to sixth grade in the old country, became a skilled welder and tradesman. He was considered non-quota. The United States exercised the non-quota stipulation because our government wanted skilled workers, not poor immigrants, especially Italians. Your grandparents had also gained U. S. citizenship, which forced Italy to let your father go because he technically then became a U.S. citizen. Your father did not fall under quota. You know your grandmother knows very little English; she worked hard, learning just the right words to pass the citizenship test. It's amazing she did that. Pretty savvy for your grandparents to figure all that out, don't you think?"

"Tell him about Mussolini. Did you tell him about Mussolini?" my father shouted.

"I will, honey," Mother replied. "When your dad thought it was a done deal and he would be heading to America, the Mussolini government suddenly confiscated his passport. Your grandparents had to hire a lawyer to get the U.S. Embassy to demand your dad's immigration. Although Mussolini grew more powerful each day, somehow America got the job done. The only thing Mussolini could do was to require your dad to complete his

Italian military service requirement before leaving."

"I saw Mussolini once," Dad shouted. "I wanted to get out of Italy even though a lot of peoples were following him. So, see? I'm not as dumb as you thinka I am."

"Jim," my mother interjected, "just remember it has not been easy for your father and the family. One of our relatives had to change their name to buy a house in a certain part of Kansas City. Your friends can quickly turn on you. Do you think your father would do that?"

My dysfunctional family, society, and a festering, big internal flaw—a sexual attraction to men—created constant turmoil in me. With his love-everybody personality, my father rose above his heritage. Known as the best welder in town, he always wanted to be first. He was the top quail hunter around and raised fine bird dogs bought by hunters from everywhere. My father always charged a fair price for his expertly trained pups and for his outstanding welding. He had his standards. Once, I remember a minister balked at the price of the weld. My father simply grabbed the work back, broke it, handed it back to him, and told the pastor to find someone else to do the job.

Dad fixed farm machinery that no one else could. Though he was the shrewdest poker player in town, he preferred playing whist, a forerunner of today's bridge. He played cards for money in the smoky back rooms of dirty bookstores in a rough area of downtown Moberly. Men affectionately called my dad "Angie," a nickname for Angelo. Women loved his wooing Italian ways and never seemed to tire of his flirting, which wasn't perceived as harassment in those days.

Dad's generosity was as limitless as the sand in the Sahara Desert. He grew an unusual Italian vegetable garden that included an enormous asparagus bed over two hundred feet long, which supplied enough crop for all of Moberly. I remember going out every day in early spring to help harvest the bounty.

"There's one over there," I would scream as I leaned over to point at a crack in the ground that exposed a spear of the crop. I balanced myself by clutching the loop on the waistline of his "unionalls."

"Thatsagooda boy," my father praised as he dug below the ground with his homemade metal picker to bring the tender white asparagus to the surface. Those were the best times in my life, but they were not destined to last.

My father loved to give his prized vegetables away to all the neighbors. Unfortunately, as I reached adolescence, I realized my friends did not appreciate the generosity.

"You'd better get your old man to stop giving us so much asparagus," my friends demanded. "It tastes horrible and makes our piss stink." Then came zucchini season. They seemed to reproduce and grow by feet overnight. Mother made boiled, fried, and sautéed zucchini with green peppers, and I really loved her fried zucchini flowers and bread.

In my friends' homes, sex was discussed in hushed tones, but my mother freely joked about it. She'd just laugh when my brother or I would swat her behind with the twirled up wet dish towel as we helped dry dishes. My mother would giggle and then scold my brother and me for our lewd antics with a zucchini.

At least once a year, my mother had the priest over for dinner. One evening, the priest excused himself to the restroom. While he was gone, my mother suddenly looked startled and then asked my father if he had taken down the nude calendar behind the bathroom door.

"Oh, shit no," my father exclaimed. Later, after the priest left, my father came from the bathroom laughing and speaking Italian. Soon my mother chuckled along with my father. My brother and I knew enough Italian to figure out the priest had flipped through the calendar and left it on the wrong month. In time, I would wonder why so many people sequestered sex, when everyone has a dirty calendar in their mind.

Kids in the neighborhood loved the perfectly constructed basketball goal my father had built in our backyard. He would sit and watch the games as he guzzled a beer before supper. My brother, despite wearing glasses, played good basketball. With disappointment in his eyes, Dad asked why I didn't play anything but an occasional game of HORSE. Sometimes he verbalized his baffled assessment of me by asking, "Why can't you be like other boys and be gooda at sports?"

My father's lack of understanding regarding my behavior chipped away at our relationship. Father had a different face at home than the happy-go-lucky attitude he displayed in public. His unending temper and tyranny would simmer and then erupt like a volcano. We never knew what would set him off. His silent treatments could last for days. I never knew how to cope with his love and hate mood swings.

As an adult, my brother concluded, "Dad tries to cover-up an inferiority complex with a superiority complex."

My father became unpredictable when he drank. As a little boy, I remember waiting for him to pick me up from school because he had stayed too long at a tavern. I would sit alone on the bicycle rack for hours after the school doors were locked. On a lucky day, he would pick me up early and take me to the saloon with him. The next day, my classmates would be jealous. I loved being the center of attention at the bar and seeing all the good-looking guys with their afternoon beard stubble. Handsome workers stirred me as they took off their hats when they entered the noisy bar. I could have as many soda pops as I wanted and always positioned the straw in my hand like men held their cigarettes. Sometimes I would get to sip the foam off of a beer. Guys would let me win at arm wrestling, and the feel of their hands in mine aroused me. My attraction to men centered on facial features, build, and masculinity. My attraction to women felt abnormal—I admired their clothes and loved the pageantry of the Miss America contest.

Playing a game on the bowling machine brought me success. I could aim and accurately throw the grapefruit-sized ball, making the plastic pins disappear upward into the machine, which indicated a strike. The tipsy guys would slap me on the back and sometimes put their caps on me. They would shout to my father, "Your boy is going to be a good bowler someday."

I would shout, "Dad, I am beating everybody." I knew from his expression that he wished that bowling were a "real" sport.

My mother tried to accentuate this more masculine endeavor by getting a neighbor to take me to the bowling alley when he took his kids for Saturday morning youth bowling while my dad was away hunting or fishing.

Moberly was a rough and redneck Midwestern city. It was founded and thrived as a railroad hub strategically located between St. Louis and Kansas City. The seedy part of town near the depot boasted more shootings, flophouses, and bars than other cities of its size. Railroaders would never tolerate a queer or anyone that was not rough and tough.

This "Magic City" had all the big chain stores and private boutiques for men and women, making it a mecca of central Missouri. There were two Catholic churches in a town of 15,000. Finally, in the 1950s, the churches consolidated in order to build a new school for grades one through ten. My parents saved earnestly to make their $350 contribution. Although catechism and Catholic doctrine filled my school days, I found that nuns and priests provided opportunities for well-rounded thinking. I read *Catcher in the Rye* while the public schools banned it, and Father Williams, my Latin teacher, loved Broadway—especially Barbra Streisand.

We owned a lower-middle-class home on the west side of town that allowed my father to run his welding business. The huge and weathered garage was adjacent to our house. Dad never fixed a broken windowpane so our mama cat could get in the garage to have kittens, which she did all the time. Dad insisted on building us a brick bungalow house while the rest of the town settled for crackerbox, ranch-style homes with single car garages.

We lived just a few hundred feet from a large set of elevated railroad tracks. Railroad lines intersected Moberly from every direction. Friends visiting us would wonder how we could tolerate the clanking sound of the freight trains with blaring whistles. My brother and I loved to watch the trains and count the number of cars as they passed by before waving at the conductor as the caboose faded into the distance. The locomotives would quickly pick up speed as they left the switchyards. I adored the art deco

13

Silverliner passenger trains that zoomed past several times a day. The dining car had a huge glass dome that exposed people eating, and I yearned to be a waiter on the train and meet people from all over the world. Other kids wanted to be engineers or switchmen.

Occasionally, a hobo would climb down from a stopped freight train and come to our back door to ask for something to eat. One day, I became irritated when my mother called me in through the front door before responding to a bum at the kitchen back door. I stomped into the kitchen, pulled the mod dinette chair from under the table, and plopped down in disgust. I didn't appreciate being interrupted when cleaning my bicycle. Mom secured the screen door with the top latch and let the hobo know she would fix something for him. Mother pulled the roasting pan from the refrigerator to prepare a roast beef sandwich.

I questioned the fate of our supper. "Mom, that's our roast beef for hash tonight!"

"I am just going to have breaded tomatoes for supper, Jim. Don't worry, there will be plenty of meat."

Watching the hobo sit in Dad's chair next to the outdoor fireplace, I told Mom that my father would not be happy. "Mom, this guy is making himself comfortable here … Gads, now he's emptying his pockets on the ledge of the fireplace." It was disgusting to watch him wet his middle fingers and paste a few strands of hair across his mostly bald head. He adjusted his jacket in preparation for the feast.

"Jimmie, I know you're mad that I interrupted your day, but if you think that I called you in because I thought you couldn't take care of yourself, you're wrong. You're getting to be a man now. Did you ever stop to think I might have called you in to protect me? Remember the other day? I had you walk on the street side of the sidewalk when we were downtown? It's what men are supposed to do to protect a lady. While we're talking, I'll tell you that you better lose your attitude. Several of your classmates have invited you over to play after school. Their mothers can drive and even have a car to bring you home. Half the time, you just come on home." Mom began to tap the butcher knife on the bottom of the sink, hard, and then harder. "You are not choosing a good path in life. A bum is a loner, too, you know."

"Why would anyone want to live like a bum? Look at his dirty clothes, he has no home and nothing good in his life," I argued.

My mother looked out the window above the kitchen sink at him and said, "Maybe he's trying to run from his past. Maybe he's searching for something he wants in life." She shrugged. "It's probably just in his bones. Who knows?" As she headed to the back door with food, she stopped and turned to me. "I just hope your father and I have taught you that you can't run from life. Your problems and who you really are will always be a step behind you."

I pointed at the bum. "Mom, that will never be me!"

CHAPTER 2

RUNAWAY

It was one of those humid, late July days in Moberly. Even at 9 or 10 years old, I hated the Midwest weather and believed there were better places to live. I had already started to manifest my self-fulfilling prophecy: to get away from the same old things of daily life, away from people teasing me about my big ears, size, and curly white-blond hair and live each day loving my lonely nature.

Mother had been nagging at me the whole day about this or that. Finally, I warned her that I might just leave home for good and catch a ride on one of the open boxcars on a freight train waiting to go somewhere to do just what I wanted.

"Mom, you're always on my back. Do this, do that. If I'm such a pain to you, maybe it would be a good idea for me to leave!"

"Well, honey, that's a great idea! In fact, I'll help you pack if you think things are so bad around here. We could have you on your way in a few minutes." Mom wasn't buying into my ability to get what I wanted out of most adults.

For as long as I could remember, I was able to flatter people and get them to love me. The lady tellers at the bank downtown always shouted greetings to me to get Mom to bring me to their window. But I could also be brutally outspoken as a child. Once an obnoxious woman commented to my mother, "When is your boy going to start to grow up? He is so small for his age!"

I snapped, "Well, I never want to grow if I grow up to be big and fat like you."

Mother had reached a point where she stopped trying to change me, and down deep inside, I knew she felt the same as I did about not taking shit off people.

There was no choice but to act on my threat to leave. Think of all the fun I'll have when there's only me to deal with. I filled my duffel bag with the essentials and some things like a favorite 78-rpm record album that I'd have no way to play on the road. Our dog, Spotty, wasn't around to pet goodbye as I headed to the back door.

"Mom, you're going to be sorry you let me go and will never find me when a freight train takes me far away."

Mother just continued to sew at the kitchen table and never gave me the satisfaction of a response. I slammed the back door and quickly trotted across the backyard onto Sturgeon Street, which could take me all the way to downtown. It was the most sordid gravel road in all of Moberly. On one side were all the railroad tracks and RR yard houses; the other side housed the poorest parts of the city. Dad often used this route to get to the city center in just about ten blocks as it angled along the tracks rather than following the grid pattern of paved residential streets. The route using normal streets was several miles more than the shortcut of Sturgeon Street.

Most of the townspeople avoided using this street because of its low-class reputation. As I walked further and further, I began to feel the uneasiness of a train that could roar past within a few feet of me at any moment. Then I cringed at life on the other side of the road. Moberly was a town of rich, upper-class railroad employees and rich store owners, doctors, and lawyers. The poorest citizens were really poor and at that age, I associated poverty with danger and being scared of their differences.

People lived in shacks and sat on their porches and walked around shirtless under their coveralls and barefoot. Outhouses were just feet from their houses and intersecting wood stakes held up long clotheslines. Despite the train smoke and dirt, their laundry looked clean and bright. Their vegetable gardens were huge and neat. The people didn't look normal to me and I was not used to seeing people with mental disabilities.

After about five blocks, I jumped across the ditch along the tracks to avoid the greasy, creosote-filled water. I kept slipping on the gravel to reach the elevated tracks above the road. I surveyed the vast number of tracks for the outgoing trains in the switchyard—there were more than I could count for as far as my eye could see. At that time of day, only a few trains sat waiting for other arrivals. I carefully dared to cross a few tracks to look inside a boxcar and see where I would sleep and live.

After finding some food, I planned to take a freight train headed in the direction past my house in order to wave goodbye to home for one last time. I finally reached the paved streets and decided to walk a few blocks to a residential area that seemed safe to approach a house to ask for some food. It was far enough from home that I felt no one would know me.

I picked a typical, brown-shingled bungalow with a small window tucked under the roof. The front porch ran the entire length of the house with the entrance at one end and a large double window perfectly centered behind the porch swing. I carefully walked up the steps onto the porch, hoping that some mean person didn't jump out and chase me away.

After just one ring, a sweet, short middle-aged lady cracked open the door. She wore black glasses tucked under grayish locks of hair pinned in a bun.

"Are you selling something, young boy?"

"No, I just left home for good and wondered if you had some cookies or something for me to eat."

After surveying me, she opened the inner door further, then unlatched the screen door and gave me the room to squeeze through. "Come in. I'll get you something and you can tell me why you are leaving home."

We walked back to the kitchen to a simple wood table sitting under a side window of the house. From the top of the shelf of the cabinet, she brought down a package of vanilla, chocolate, and strawberry cream-filled wafer cookies. Soon, I was munching on wafers and milk.

"What's your name, young man?" she asked.

"I'm Jim."

"Do you have a last name?"

"I am not tellin'."

"Oh, I see. It sounds like you are really serious about leaving home. Do you have any money in your pockets?"

"I took my savings and that's it."

"Well, I'll tell you what, I'm going to find you some change. You'll need a lot of money to get by."

She returned with several pennies and nickels in a small, red plastic coin purse that opened with a side squeeze. "Here is some money, and my name and phone number are on this piece of paper. You can call me from anywhere and can ask the operator to ask me to accept charges and then she will put you through. OK?"

Before I had finished my snack, the front doorbell ding-donged. I looked from the kitchen table through the dining room and out the big window of the front room to see two policemen waiting on the porch. *Darn it, she called the police on me!*

When she went to answer the door, I tiptoed to the back door and turned the round deadbolt to open the door. It was hard to turn, but within a few tries, I was off the back porch and ran across several backyards before coming to a car parked in a driveway. I crouched under its big front bumper and looked down the side of the car until I saw the police car drive past. I slowly walked out to the corner of the house, so that I could watch the squad car enter the next block.

I charged to the intersection and ran hard down the new street to outsmart the cops. By this time, I had to pee. A couple of houses down, big evergreens alongside a huge two-story house provided the perfect place to go. Just as I put my *tigga* back in my pants, a huge hand grabbed my shirt collar. A policeman had me, and the heels of my shoes skidded across the yard as he pulled me onto the gravel driveway.

"What are you doing, boy!" one of the two policemen shouted. "You can't piss there. You're in big trouble."

The older cop dragged me toward the cherry-topped police car as the other cop opened the back door so the one holding me by the arms and shoulders could throw me in the backseat. This was not going to be the last time for that experience.

"What's your name kid?" The older cop asked.

"James Rostello," I said.

"So, you're Angelo and Irene's son?"

The other policeman added, "Yeah, I've seen him in the neighborhood." He turned to me and said, "You're not going to hear the end of this. You want to grow up and be a bum? How did you get this far from home? Son, you are on the wrong path in life. This is how criminals are made."

Little more was said by anyone on the drive home. Mom thanked the policemen and didn't even cry for joy that I was okay. Everything just went on like nothing happened except that things were very quiet. As Dad sat down to eat, he warned, "You better never do this to your mom again, you little shit."

As always, the next Sunday in church, Mom reached for her little alabaster case and pulled out the beautiful ruby red beads that I had always admired, and she began to pray. When I opened my mother's purse after she died, that rosary case was still there after more than 30 years. As I touched the beautiful red rosary inside, it dawned on me; ruby was my birthstone.

CHAPTER 3

A MOTHER'S EAR

Sometimes, when my father had some extra money and was in a good mood, we would go to Dairy Queen for treats. One evening when I was around 12 years old, I became excited when I saw Dad put on his cap and ask Mom if she wanted to go out for a drive and stop for ice cream.

Mom and Dad waited in the car after ordering their favorite: a pineapple ice cream sundae. Standing at the service window, I spied an order of crispy, crinkle-cut French fries coming out of the fryer. *Boy, I wish Mom could make French fries like that.*

I rushed to the car and asked Dad if I could have French fries instead of ice cream. "It's only 25 cents more," I pleaded.

"Get whatever you think you want," Dad said, looking away from me and over to Mom as I hurried back to the counter to place my order. I couldn't wait to begin eating them after I jumped into the back seat.

Nothing was said during the ride home, an omen that things were not okay with my father's mood. Intent on enjoying my fries, I ignored the warning signs. When we got home, Dad slammed the car door and charged into the house.

What's going on? I gave back the change from the French fries. What did I do this time?

As I entered the house via the back door, the volcano erupted.

My father was more enraged than I could ever remember. "What'sa the fuck is wrong with you, you stupid little son of a beech. Your mom anda me had a wonderful pineapple ice creama sundae that'sa good for you, and you have God-damns greasy Frencha fries."

My dad pulled a cold French fry out of his pocket. He had asked me for one on the way home.

As he tried to force-feed it to our French poodle, he screamed, "Looka here, the dog won't even eat this piece of shit." As he turned and started to walk away, I made the fatal mistake of sticking my tongue out at him. He turned around and caught me. I knew immediately the consequence would be grave.

Never having seen my father this mad in all my life, I quickly took refuge under the kitchen table. As he reached under the table to pull me out of my protected center spot, I used one of the chairs tucked under the table as a shield; he took the chair and violently threw it against the kitchen cabinets. Then, I produced another chair. He ran to the other side of the table, and I moved enough to avoid his reach again. He threw another chair the full length of the kitchen.

My father stormed toward the back door with his edict, "You will notta leave this house and yardda for one weeks, and you will notta have no treats, dezzert, or sweets of any kind, and no visitors or TV." Given my father's Italian temper, I knew him giving the silent treatment to the entire family, and his glassy blue eyes constantly staring at me, would be the icing on the cake of punishment.

Three days later when Dad had finally cooled off enough to speak to me, he "blessed" me with a perplexing story. As his anger grew, his Italian accent became more slurred as he lectured me.

"I have to get you to see why I need to kick your ass sometimes. There was once a mother back in Italia who never punished her son and protected him when he did wrong. He would steal and break the law, but she always said he didn't do it and blamed other people. She would say her son did nothing bad. One day, he robbed a grocery store and shot and killed the owner, even as the innocent man did everything he wanted.

"While waiting to be hung from the big old tree in the center of the prison yard, the evil son's last request was to see his mother so he could whisper in her ear his last thoughts and then kiss her goodbye.

"'See how much my son loves his mother and respects me,' his mother bragged to the old Padre and prison executor when she heard his request. 'He wants to tell me how much he loves me for the good mother I have been and all I have done for him.'

"'Come closer, so I can whisper to you privately,' the young man pleaded, his hands bound in chains to the chair.

"As she leaned her face close to her son, he instantly pulled himself and the chair off the floor and lunged at her ear. With a quick jerk, he grabbed her ear with his teeth. He bit harder and harder until her ear lodged in his teeth and blood dripped from his mouth. Then, he spit her ear on the floor.

"'That's for not being a loving mom and teaching me right from wrong,' the young man angrily shouted to his mother.

"This is why, son, you must be punished good when you have been a bad boy," my father scolded.

"What in the world does this have to do with me?" I pleaded. "I just ordered French fries instead of ice cream with your okay, Dad. I'm not a thief or murderer."

My father became enraged. His face turned bright red and his blue eyes darted back to Mom, who was standing in the hallway. She kept her face down, shaking her head in fear.

He began shouting and screaming. "Me and your mother justa don't understand you! You're such a weirda boy that never listens or actsa like a man. We don'ta know howa to handle you anymore." He slammed the back door so hard as he stormed out that the glass broke in the windowpane.

That day, I saw a side of my father I would never understand, and I felt like a bad son, a scoundrel. To this day, I carry the story of that mother's ear in the back of my mind. There were few bridges of understanding between my father and me.

Many years later, I stood in the vestibule of the local Catholic funeral home chapel, waiting with my mother and brother to see my father as he lay in state. As the funeral director ushered us in and down the aisle, I slowed my pace and stopped several yards from the open casket, barely able to see my father.

"Come close to your father," my mother encouraged me from alongside the beautiful bronze casket. "Your father looks so peaceful. He won't suffer from those horrible heart attacks anymore. He is with God. We will miss him so," Mom cried.

I looked down at the red velvet carpet and drew a bit closer, pretending to acknowledge my father so as to please my mother. I held my head down while we sat in the front pew waiting to begin praying the rosary.

Questions and thoughts started running through my mind:

Why didn't I cry when I remembered all the times my father would hold a shiny quarter a bit too high for me to grab, lowering it until I could reach it?

Why didn't I cry when I remembered being 5 or 6 and my father would lay on his back on the floor and lift me high into the air, my feet secured in his hands as I struggled to hold my balance, screaming in the joy of my accomplishment? We were going to be the main attraction in the circus and travel the world!

Why didn't I cry when standing next to Mom in front of the casket while everyone passed by saying how much they loved Angelo and would miss him? One of my father's friends, the owner of the local auto parts store, began to sob when he told Mom that everyone always knew their day would suddenly get better when their Italian buddy entered the room.

Why didn't I cry, knowing he was gone forever from my life?

Why didn't I cry when I looked down at my black rosary while praying and remembered "A Mother's Ear"?

Why didn't I cry when I realized that bad had won the battle over good and would haunt the closets of my heart?

CHAPTER 4

BEAT UP AND SENT TO MY ROOM

Possessing less athletic ability than other children got me into trouble when I was younger. It took me longer than the other boys to ride a bike. Happiness filled my life when my training wheels finally came off, allowing me to explore the world far from home. Soon after that happened, I discovered my second great love in life, after helping Mom cook, when I found a flower nursery six blocks away.

The owner of the nursery let me cut off old rose blooms, water some plants, and eat Red Hots hidden on the top shelf above the cash register. All the ladies loved when I carried their flower purchases to their cars and sent them off with a big hug and kiss. Mr. Dougherty actually said one day, "You are damn good for business."

Being only 11 years old, the nurseryman would pay me with nearly dead flowers, which I brought home to prosper. One day, he sent me away with a beautiful, potted geranium, that I immediately gave to my mother. When Dad came home from work, she quickly let him know that at least one man in her life gave her flowers, pointing at the plant on the kitchen table.

In his heavy Italian accent, Dad began to curse. "Sumina-beech, holy sheet. First, my boy likes to cook, now he likes flowers? I needa a fucking beer. I'ma going to Bud's tavern. Don't waits fora me to eatta supper."

Our hunting dogs, Picca (pronounced Peeka) and Brownie rousted around their pen, anxiously waiting for their supper and freedom to run in the yard. After they watched my father drive away, they laid down with disappointment in their eyes.

One beautiful, mid-spring day, the school bus ground to a halt in front of our home. I charged off the bus into the house to have my Tang and melted peanut butter on toast so I could head to the nursery and see if the new rose bushes were in.

"Before you run off, Jim, you need to go to the grocery store. We're having fried chicken for supper. Oh, and take the list I made out, I need that woman thing. I put it on the list so you don't have to ask for it."

Darn it, I can remember an eight to ten item grocery list with no problem. I even know the top ten cities in the U.S. and the world and their exact populations. Mom knows that. This could only mean one thing. She wants that girly stuff: Kotex.

I hurriedly rode up the street and over one block to the neighborhood grocery where Mom ran a tab. I dutifully presented the list and slipped to the side of the counter near the candy case. Good ole Mr. Redmond knocked down a box of Kotex from a high shelf in the back of the store. He flipped it high in the air and then caught it between the palms of his hands several times. Then, he tossed the powder blue box on the counter next to the rest of the items on the list with a sarcastic snicker. Another shopper, cranky old widow Mrs. "Nosy," inspecting the items on the counter, commented to Mrs. Redmond with a disapproving glare at me, "Are those his groceries?"

I grabbed the sack of groceries and bolted out the big screen door, throwing it open by forcefully pushing its big, metal Coca-Cola medallion handle and running out.

"Don't slam the door," Mrs. Redmond shouted.

As I pushed my bicycle out onto the main sidewalk, groceries in one hand and the other on the handlebars, the day suddenly took a turn for the worst. I saw big bad bully, Kenny Petry, standing at the end of the block, right where I was headed. I looked the other direction, thinking of going home an opposite route. The meanest of his accomplices, Steve, stood there glaring at me on the opposite corner.

Oh my God. He can't see me with this Kotex. He'll kill me!

I stopped and dropped the bike from under me as I dashed back into the store, throwing the unwanted box onto the counter. "Darn, Mr. Redmond, I forgot to tell you that Mom told me to scratch the Kotex off the list because she wouldn't be needing it now."

Several shoppers quickly joined Mr. and Mrs. Redmond in a big discussion. As I ran out the door, they started giggling. When I reached the point where Kenny waited for me on his bike, he forced me to stop and face him.

"Ah, little Jimmie-Joe finally got his training wheels off," he said, pushing his front bike wheel against mine.

By this time, Steve had my back wheel pinned. "Yeah, little fairy flower boy is grocery shopping for his mommy."

With one push from Kenny, my front tire and handlebars flipped under me, crashing me down to the oil and rock-paved street. Half-oiled rocks pierced my hand while my elbows and arms scraped across the road. My groceries—a frying chicken, onions and potatoes, bananas, bread, and milk—flew in all directions. In all my pain, I was glad Kotex did not appear on the street.

"Next time we get you, you'll be dead meat," Kenny shouted as he and Steve rode away.

I quickly charged home, hid the groceries under the evergreens in the front of the house, and ran inside. "I fell off my bike. I'll get to the store as soon as I get some iodine and Band-Aids," I told Mom.

Mom just muttered as she read the evening paper, "You're sure taking a long time."

I snuck into my bedroom, grabbed up all the coins sitting on top of the dresser, emptied my money jar and hid the money in my pockets. I hurried out the door in the opposite direction to the other neighborhood store. It was a small market sided in red asphalt shingles with a sheet metal roof.

Thank goodness there were only two customers in the store. I slipped behind the bread counter and grabbed a box of Kotex. The old, creaky wooden floor gave me away to everyone. I walked up to the counter with the dreaded box and tossed every cent of my money—all in pennies, nickels, a few dimes, and a quarter— on the counter.

"Geez," Mr. Willard mumbled. "Hard times at your house? Your mom needs you to buy this? Don't know if you have enough money here."

"Mr. Willard, don't blame my mom. I told her I wanted to get this for her because she needed it. Men are supposed to take care of their moms."

"Well, you're a good boy. Tell you what, let's just call this an even purchase. Go get yourself a Chocolate Soldier from the pop case."

"Hot-diggity dog-ziggity," I shouted, skipping to the back of the store for my chocolate flavored soda. I pulled an icy-cold bottle of my favorite drink from the cooler.

My day was finally working out. I ran home quickly to combine all the groceries from both stores before going inside. Checking out the new shipment of rose bushes would have to wait until the next day. Mom's lard-fried chicken, mashed potatoes and milk gravy, salt-pork green beans, and banana pudding with vanilla wafers made everything okay.

The next day, the school bus reached my house a bit later than usual. Butterball, our rescued farm cat, waited in the driveway with her question mark tail waving as I bolted off the bus. I gave her a quick pet. She began to purr and rubbed against my legs as she followed me to the front door. After my snack, I would be off to the nursery.

When I entered the front door of our house, Mom was standing in the foyer; one hand in each of her apron pockets, I knew this was a bad sign.

"Jim, what's the big idea of telling all the neighbors you're going to have a new brother or sister? It's bad enough that you tell all the neighborhood biddies how much our water and light bills are. Now you tell them I'm having a baby? A 42-year-old woman having a baby? I'm the talk of the town. Go straight to your room right now, and don't come out till supper."

"Mom, I didn't tell anyone that you were going to have a baby." Only later in life would I realize what the adults at the store assessed from my return of the Kotex. I slowly baby-stepped to my room. Before I could shut the door, Mom grabbed the knob on the opposite side and slammed it closed like a hurricane wind.

I flopped down and buried my face on my Roy Rogers bedspread. Beat up and sent to my room, all in two days!

CHAPTER 5

GOBBO

How much will it hurt? Will I feel awful when it's over?

H A car ride to the dentist or doctor seemed so quick when I wanted time to be my friend. The familiar neighborhood and city landmarks flashed by until I reached the dreaded destination.

From the living room window, I watched the taxi pull into our driveway on a late spring day. Mom opened the taxi's back door and motioned for me to get in. She adjusted her dress before sitting down in the front seat. My thoughts centered on my failure and the disappointment I had caused my parents. At just around 12 years old, I had failed to be a good, controllable son.

They're ashamed to call me a Rostello. Maybe it would be better if they just sent me away.

Many times, after they went to bed, they would talk loud enough for me to hear. They contemplated sending me far from home to a mental institution or boys' school.

I would hear my father demand to my mother, "Let's don't chickens outta in doing the right thing iffa Jim doesn't shapes up and fly right."

The library had provided me with a great deal of information about the worst alternative, Fulton Missouri State Mental Hospital. Meals and daily life would be on a rigid schedule. I cringed at the pictures of huge pills I would never be able to swallow. Daily rules and procedures would be followed exactly, and my behavior would be monitored and recorded until I changed from bad to good.

The picture of the electric shock chair and a straitjacket I saw when reading about mental institutions frightened me so vividly that I had to quickly flip those pages.

No more days at St. Pius X School.
No more of Grandma Rosalia's homemade gnocchi.
No more afternoons teaching geography to our cats and dogs.
No more monopoly with my brother Albert.
No more of anything I enjoyed in life.

My research led me to a full-page black and white picture of this dark and dreary mental hospital. Big ornate gates hid the huge foreboding art deco structure that promised total isolation. Everything about the place appeared petrifying, lonely, and made me think of the other troubled children who would torment me every day.

One day at the library while I was looking at the picture of the hospital for the hundredth time, the head librarian, Mrs. Bentley, tapped me on the shoulder.

"James, why are you looking at pictures of such a depressing place? That's a place I hope you'll never go."

"Mrs. Bentley, I'm not a very good son. I disappoint my mother and father more than I please them."

"Well, James, you shouldn't worry about that. I think you're a good boy. I've watched you studying and reading many times right over there by that big window. You have good manners and a good mind. Your parents will protect you and keep you away from that place."

If she only knew. I nodded as she rambled on with the encouragement. *She doesn't know the truth about things within me: I'm queer.*

The information on admission requirements and patient profiles from mental hospitals clearly used that dreaded word, homosexual. Sexual deviancy, sometimes a characteristic of mental patients, could be a reason for being committed to an institution in those days.

That day, my mom was reluctantly taking me to the doctor for my undesirable posture and moodiness. *But what if they find out I'm queer? What if they send me away? Does Mom know I've had sex with other boys?*

A mentally retarded man from our church had been arrested for being homosexual and had been committed to a mental hospital.

Would they really send me away?

As the old Nash Taxi backed into the street, I hung on to the old velour rope handle attached to the back of the front seat. "Dr. Cains' office," my mother instructed.

The cab driver, 'Beans,' turned to talk to me in the back seat, "Is my buddy Jim not feeling good today?"

Before I could answer, my mother changed the conversation to the dark June thunderstorm that brewed in the west.

My thoughts shifted to how embarrassing it must be for a mother to take her son to the doctor for slumped shoulders. As the taxi pulled away, I began to list all of the things I didn't like about myself.

Passing the beautiful, manicured corner home of Mrs. Holland a few blocks up Emerson Street:

I have big ears. Dad must have heard me called "elephant ears." He made me wear a cut out band of my mother's stocking hose around my ears and head to train my ears to lay back.

My big, green bug eyes.

Stupid platinum blond extra curly hair. That's not ideal for a boy.

Ten blocks from home at the four-way stoplight that blinked red:

I am terrible at sports, except bowling, which isn't a real sport according to Dad; what a disappointment to a dad to never see his

son play Little League.
I love to cook.
I love flowers.
I hate hunting and killing animals.

Passing the bakery on the edge of downtown and looking up 5th Street to Main Street and the big department store:

Every year I make Mom take me to the girl's toy section at Christmastime to decide on the cooking set I want. How embarrassing for both of us.
I always pester my teachers to grade papers and practice piano after school.
I hate my nickname, "Jimmie Joe."

Traveling down the business highway:

I love to hang around the ladies in the neighborhood while they fix supper. Virginia is my favorite. I sit on a stool in her kitchen as she prepares dinner, and we discuss things like which was more efficient: peeling a potato with a paring knife or using a potato peeler.
School is great. I adore reading and writing, my penmanship is better than most girls.

Passing the hospital where I was born, next door to the doctor's office:

I love everything about houses, especially design, furniture, decorating.
I cry way too easy—especially during sad movies.

Pulling up in front of the medical clinic:

And the winner! I'm queer. I like boys.

Alice, my favorite nurse, greeted me with her usual hug as we entered the clinic. She smelled so good. She held me close to her waist. Classiness oozed from her statue-like face and steel-gray bird's nest hairstyle. I loved her. She could give me a shot so that it didn't hurt a bit.

After a few minutes, she called us into Dr. Cain's office. Mom played with the clasp on her purse, moving it from side to side as we waited for the doctor. We didn't talk to each other. Like most doctors, Dr. Cain entered the room reading my chart. He put a big X-ray photo on the light standing near his desk to have another look. It had been taken a week earlier at the hospital.

"Nothing wrong on the X-rays of your spine, Jim," the doctor announced. "So, tell me. Why don't you stand up straighter? It would make your appearance better."

"Doctor, I don't feel like standing up straight and tall. It's a feeling type of thing, I think. Like maybe I wish I weren't around."

"Hogwash," my mother blurted out. "You're just being lazy, and it's a bad habit. God has given you a wonderful body, and you need to take care of how you stand."

Dr. Cain sat silently for a moment then looked at me over the top of his glasses while addressing my mother, "We can get him a back brace and see if that helps, Irene." Then he said to me, "In the meantime, Jim, try to stand up straight. It'll make your parents happy."

Standing in front of the clinic and waiting for the taxi to take us home, I tried to deny the day's dejection while licking the grape sucker I had just received. I secured my grip on it by wrapping my fingers inside the looped string handle. My mother brushed my hair back with her fingers.

"Jim, let me tell you something. As a young girl in my twenties, men used to whistle at me and catcall me all the time because of my big bust. I ignored them, threw my shoulders back, and was proud of what God had given me in a time when being flat-chested was popular. Please try and do better with your posture for me. This really bothers your father, and I don't want to see you in a back brace."

At the supper table that night, my father was not happy.

The easy solution he had hoped for from the doctor had not materialized.

Gazing out the window at Picca and Brownie and taking a long drink from his 16-ounce mega can of Schlitz beer, he looked at me with his decision, "I guessa we needa to start calling you a gobbo. It's an Italian guy that walksa around like he issa scared of everyones, slump-shouldered and notta proud to be a man."

My brother, sitting across the table, began to chuckle. "My brother is a gobbo—that's funny. Hi, gobbo!" Albert now had a perfect way to get under my skin, but thankfully he could only use it when we were home with the family. He did not want other guys knowing about the Italian sayings we used at home.

So, for years to follow, whenever Dad became frustrated with my posture, he would shout, "Stand up straight, gobbo!"

I hated myself more and more. I am still gobbo today despite now knowing the power that low self-esteem can have on what we say, the ways we act, and how we carry ourselves. I will take the word "gobbo" and gobboness to my deathbed.

CHAPTER 6

WHIPPED CREAM AND PUMPKIN PIE

Father always drove to Centerville, Iowa, about eighty miles north of Moberly, to pick up Grandpa Felice and Grandma Nona just a few days before Christmas. Mom always wanted the Christmas tree decorated before they arrived, and it would be Dad's first day off for the holiday.

Nona always made pasta when she visited because my mother never had the touch of making wonderful thin noodles. Grandma would start by breaking one egg into a ravine she had made in the mound of flour. With a fork, she'd beat the egg until the flour slowly integrated. Then, she would bring it into a ball and knead it carefully, folding it over and over. She worked on the edge of our big, 1950s dinette table. Mom would open the closet and bring her a special tool: an old, window shade spring roller that allowed you to adjust the shade to any position and darken and bring privacy to the bedroom. The ripped shade had been removed, and now the long, wooden roller belonged to Nona's artisan hands. She would expand the dough slowly from the center, turning the pasta around and around as she wrapped the pasta around the pin and then laid it back down. With my legs and feet tucked under me, I sat at the dinette side chair watching the pasta dough grow little by little.

By the time Nona finished, the almost-see-through pasta

covered the entire table. Then came the fun. Grandma would roll up the big circle of dough into a long tube and cut off small sections. I would grab each one quickly by the end and lift it up in the air and watch a perfect noodle unfold as it dropped to the table. By then, Mom would have made my bed and laid a clean, white sheet on the bedspread. Nona would spread the noodles out to dry before the noon meal.

Grostoli only happened at Christmas and it had the same procedure as noodles except right after the egg was broken into the flour hole, Mom would bring the whiskey bottle and add a generous pour of this secret ingredient. Nona would roll out the pasta into an unusually huge circle. Instead of cutting the rolled-up pasta into segments to become noodles, I was summoned to the table to cut up the huge surface into different shapes and sizes. Then, Mom would heat oil in the big skillet, and I would watch the dough explode into puffed up shapes with gigantic air pockets as she carefully slipped the intoxicated pasta pieces into the grease. I always screamed with joy and clapped. Then the hot grostoli would go to the butcher block cutting area and be sprinkled with sugar. Hence, came Nona's grostoli.

• • •

Struggles with my parents, social isolation, and a prescribed Catholic morality defined my childhood. My early teen years were miserable, unhappy, and self-conscious. Homosexual thoughts alienated me from the Catholic Church and God, leaving me caged by loneliness and despair.

The daily catechism classes in grade school always identified me as a sinner. In the fourth grade, Sister Hermenia spoke directly to my flawed relationship with God when she said, "If you miss Mass on Sunday or engage in impure thoughts and actions and die without confessing those mortal sins, you will burn in Hell for eternity."

I knew nuns and priests would vehemently oppose the beginning of my homosexual tendencies and self-engaged misconduct. The thought of the priest finding out about my behavior loomed over me, making a good confession and a Holy Communion impossible.

> Stumbling through childhood, one day I tripped over a
>> warped sidewalk that had been heaved by the roots
>> of a huge oak tree.
> As I lay on the pavement, scratched, and bruised inside
>> and out, my eyes took me under the barren hedge
>> to a lovely rockfish pond.
> A fair-haired boy sat in solitude on the water's edge,
>> tossing wishes on sticks at the wandering koi.
> Without an overture, he looked over to me.
>> His contagious giggle eased my embarrassment
>> and kindled admiration and excitement.
> Bobby's straight, fawn-colored hair dangled beneath
>> his bright red ball cap.
> His robin's egg-blue eyes darted with his spontaneous
>> laughter.
> He was 13, only about a year older than me,
>> when love nurtured our hearts.
> We played and explored the summer days in friendship.
> The touch of his smooth body and supple groin opened
>> wondrous dimensions for me.

My road to Hell began after my summer of sin following sixth grade when I met Bobby. As the summer progressed, we engaged in childhood sexual intimacy. A couple of years later, he moved away. He left me alone on life's train when the August rains began.

Going back to school meant the return of confession and Communion. As I waited in the line of boys kneeling in alphabetical order in the pew, I watched the red light above the confessional click on and off each time a boy entered and exited the room.

How am I going to tell the priest that I've had sex with a boy? Then tell him exactly what happened? Will Father know who I am by looking through the frosted plastic window? What would be worse: the scolding, damnation, or the amount of penance?

When my turn finally arrived, I genuflected as I left the pew and walked hesitantly into the confessional. I pulled the confessional door closed after entering, holding the knob stationary then slowly releasing until the door latched. I continued into the confessional holding my head down and eased my knees onto the bright red knee bench.

I looked into the window. *Oh my God, it's Monsignor. That window isn't worth shit; I know who he is, and he knows who I am. I'm in so much trouble! Holy Jesus, why did I do those things with Bobby? God, please help me!*

"Bless me, Father, for I have sinned. It's been three months since my last confession."

"Continue, my son."

"Father, I fought with my brother, missed several Sunday Masses, sassed my mother and father, and said some cuss words." I paused. "For these and all my sins, I am sorry." Within a moment, my chance to tell the truth was gone.

"You must honor your father and mother as a commandment of God and come to church every Sunday. I don't want to hear these sins again. Say fifteen Hail Marys, fifteen Our Fathers, and ten Glory Be to the Fathers as your penance. Now say your Act of Contrition."

My fate was sealed. I muttered the Act of Contrition without thinking about the words. My thoughts centered on getting hit by a car and going straight to Hell.

I rose to my feet and tiptoed out of the confessional, meticulously shutting the door behind me. As I walked down the aisle, a stream of amber light from my favorite stained-glass window, high in the ceiling gable, caught the side of my face and the back of the pews. The smiling face of Jesus looked at me with love and compassion. Frisky little puppies joyfully played at Christ's feet.

The dogma of the Catholic Church had created enormous stress for me, making me believe that I was possessed by the devil.

As I kneeled in a pew to begin my fake penance, the smile of the Son of God turned to disappointment and lost love. His eyes pierced my heart and soul with rejection. The puppies transformed into growling little wolves nipping at Jesus's feet. As the sun set, the sunlight filtered through the stained-glass disappeared, and the puffy white clouds became blue-black in a brewing storm.

With the confessions completed, daily Mass began. Soon it would be time for Holy Communion. Taking Communion with mortal sin on your soul was the greatest sacrilege. The complete death of the soul. A first-class ticket to Hell.

Oh my God, please help me!

As my row filed out of the pew and each of us headed to the Communion rail, I prayed for the courage not to take it. It seemed like the walk was over in a flash with no chance to turn back. I knelt on the hard, wooden floor in front of the rail and rested my hands on the pure white ceremonial cloth, my hands clasped in prayer.

As the priest moved down the line of boys toward me, I could feel each beat of my heart and relive each moment of homosexual sin in my mind.

What? The Priest is looking for unbroken hosts in the chalice! Jim, God is sending you the help you prayed for! When he was just two boys away from me, the Priest turned and darted from the boy next to me back to the altar for more hosts. I was granted more time to think.

I got it! When he gets to you, just close your eyes and make the sign of the cross like you have the host in your mouth. Then get up and walk away. No one can see in front of you. This will work.

The priest moved swiftly down the altar steps, his ivory cloak trailing behind him. Within a second, he was standing in front of me. He lifted up a perfect white host and waited for me to open my mouth and take the body of Christ.

Instantly, the host was on my tongue, and I had committed the greatest of sins. Back in the pew, the most reverent boys buried their heads in their hands to pray. I hid my face between my partially open fingers, looking straight down to Hell.

The old adage that problems are sometimes solved by others or events worked for me regarding Communion. With a fasting rule that required Catholics eat no food after midnight the night before receiving the body of Christ, I was able to use my mom as an excuse to not take Communion at school. She hated fixing breakfast for me to eat after Communion at school.

Although I envied the other kids who got to eat breakfast during class after Mass, I was relieved I didn't have to commit that mortal sin daily.

The Church eventually relaxed the fasting rules to just three hours before Communion. The school moved Mass to just before lunch. Without a valid excuse, I was backed into a corner. I could feel the Sisters glaring at me when I remained in the pew during Communion.

One day while working on math, I looked down to see the perfectly tied black shoes of Sister Mary Agnes. She tapped me on the shoulder.

"James, why do you choose to not take the body and blood of Christ?"

"Sister, there are so many times I just don't feel holy or worthy to receive God."

A big smile lit up her strict face. "Jim, you must take Christ more often. Just say some extra prayers, and you will feel more holy for the most important thing in life."

I was proud of myself. Technically, I'd told the truth and earned some brownie points, too.

During daily Mass, I prayed for a change in my sinful life. Again, the actions of others gave me an opportunity to get right with God. Dad always insisted on driving to a nearby town for his confession at Christmas and Easter. I wondered why he just did not want to go to our local church. Were his sins that bad? Usually, my brother and I would stay in the car and play checkers while Dad and Mom trekked inside for confession, but I knew that this was my only chance to tell my mortal sins without anyone knowing who I was.

"Mom, I cussed during recess the other day at school. I need to see the priest before Christmas Communion." I knew my story was sold when I saw Mom look at Dad and wink.

"OK. Come along, Jim. Albert, you can come inside, too, and say some extra prayers."

"Way to go, dickhead!" Albert scolded me behind my parents' backs as we headed inside the church.

Although the anticipation of confession scared me, I was focused on redemption. Maybe God is taking my hand this time. I almost slammed the confessional door. Kneeling down, I looked up to another worthless, mostly translucent plastic window. The priest had curly black hair. A bright purple confessional stole dangled over his shoulders.

"Bless me Father, for I have sinned. It's been a week since my last confession. I cussed at my brother, didn't obey my parents, and lied to a friend." Then, in a muted tone, I said, "Father, I committed fornication with a neighbor boy then made some bad confessions and took Communion." The silence that followed seemed never-ending.

My best-laid plans began to fail. In a heavy Irish accent, the priest demanded, "We need to go somewhere and talk. You have fallen into grave sin."

Shit, he's going to haul me out of here in front of my parents!

"Father, you have a lot of people lined up waiting for confession. I just moved here and will be attending school at St. Joseph's here in Salisbury right after Christmas vacation. I can come to the rectory then and we can talk and pray."

After a short interlude, he looked at his watch and whispered, "For your penance, say five Our Fathers and five Hail Marys. Now pray hard for God to forgive you and guide you away from sin."

Damn, it worked! I am a good performer on my knees.

Christmas Day was the best day of my life. My gifts of new cooking utensils could not match the relief in my mind. I buried my head in my hands just like the other boys did in joyful prayer. Holiness filled my soul.

The following summer, the neighborhood's paper delivery boy, John, offered me a helper position. I was his first choice among all the guys. Everyone had vied for the job. God was rewarding me for my new path in life. This was big stuff: $6.25 per week!

"Let's go to my clubhouse and decide on your portion of my route," John suggested one day.

We ventured down the neighborhood creek ravine through thick brush and small trees to the opening to his secret hideaway. I hurried along as quickly as he did in a state of blissful excitement. Looking up to the blue sky in his cleared spot among the weeds and trees seemed so neat.

John walked over, grabbed me from behind, held my waist in his arms, reached around, and unzipped my shorts. Then, he walked in front of me and pulled out my penis. On his knees, he began to give me oral sex. It felt good, and, by this time, I noticed that he was nicely endowed. I became excited. Within a few minutes, I ejaculated for the first time in my life. As soon as I comprehended what had happened, I ran home, jumped in the bathtub, and washed every inch of my body.

I was a sinner again, going right back to making bad confessions and Communions. My conscience tormented me. Making amends with God was not a possibility.

One day, standing next to my dresser in front of the window in my bedroom, I picked up a little plastic chapel containing the Virgin Mary, her hands outstretched. It was a first Communion gift that had cost my parents $3.50. As I stood in front of my bedroom window, the sultry July heat drifted into the room. I held the icon to my chest and began to pray for Mary to bring me forgiveness from God and change me into a better person.

As I gazed out to the gravel road running alongside my home, Lonny, a young neighbor man came to his car to leave for work. He worked as a prison guard, and his uniform was pressed to perfection. His curly blond hair was cut high and tight on his handsome, blushy face. With the Virgin Mary statue in hand, I began to lust for Lonny. An intense desire to be naked with him filled my thoughts.

I'm a sick little fucker. How can I be praying and thinking about sex with a man at the same time? I am not fit to be part of this earth.

Why can't I just die?

In a swift movement with my hand, I opened the plastic lattice doors to the little chapel, grabbed them in haste, forcibly yanked both doors off, and threw them on the floor. I can't remember my feelings at that moment. Realizing what I had just done, tears streamed down my cheeks. I opened the bottom dresser drawer and hid the broken doors and the little chapel behind some clothes I never wore. Jesus, Mary, and God were at that moment gone from my life.

My life was a living hell filled with unhappiness and guilt. Those feelings were like whipped cream on a slice of pumpkin pie: continually stacking up until I could no longer find my soul. I could find nothing in my life that was good. I was an embarrassment to my father, a burden to my brother, a challenge for my mother, and an abomination to my God. There was only one person in my life that I loved and who loved me unconditionally: Grandma Nona.

I began to unravel. Mom was uptown, and my father, grandfather, and brother were hunting, which left me alone with my grandmother. I lay on my bed in the fetal position, crying and begging to die. I rolled over, facing the entrance to my bedroom. Grandmother was standing in the hallway watching me. One hand clutched her cleavage, and the other tightly gripped her ankle-length flowery apron. Her huge chestnut eyes were sullen and teary. She did not know a single word of English. Her eyes did all the talking:

"Where is that happy little boy that used to ride piggyback on me, screaming in laughter as I carried you throughout the house? I have always loved you and always will love you." She walked to the side of my bed and reached out to hold me.

"Go away … go away!" Nona did not surrender. She moved closer to the bed. I felt her pushing against the mattress as her timeworn, withered hand touched my side just above my waist. I understood her first two words, "Bello bambino." Neither her sobbing in Italian nor the pain showing on her 87-year-old sweet face was able to corral or calm my crying rampage.

"Go away, dammit. I said go away! I don't love you anymore. I don't love anyone anymore," I screamed.

I turned over, facing the wall again. I had no more tears to cry. I heard Grandma slowly shuffle away, leaving me alone. The last person that truly loved me was removed from my life. The destruction of my life was complete.

Since I could trust no one with my childhood secrets, translating my regrets into Italian for Grandma was never possible. She would have understood and accepted me. I pray Nona did not die thinking I didn't love her with all my heart because of the day I rejected her. I often contemplate that some things in life should not be said, some things need not be said, and some things must be said.

Grandma, I miss your grostoli de Nona.

Nona, I love you.

CHAPTER 7

SIDEWAYS AND DOWN

When I was in my very early teens, I would sit atop the kitchen table, chatting about my favorite movies as Mother prepared dinner. Mom always took me to the cinema on Sunday afternoons while Dad hunted or fished with my older brother.

One late winter afternoon, I was drawing sketches with my finger on the steamy window above the table: a playbill of Rock Hudson and Doris Day in "Lover Come Back." Mom's minestrone in progress always made the glass a perfect opaque surface.

"Rock Hudson is a good actor." I hesitated, really wanting to say I thought he was handsome. However, I knew a man is never supposed to comment on another man's good looks. I was scared and not secure enough to say that Hudson was homosexual. Just saying that word was bad in those days.

My mother stared away from me. She carefully continued to scrape carrot stalks with her butcher knife above the kitchen sink. In a serious tone, she said, "They say he's a 'homosexall' and that's a very bad, sinful thing."

Why can't my mother say the word 'homosexual' right?

I remember gazing out the window and feeling like one of the huge fluffy-white snowflakes that was hitting the window, turning to a big drop of water, running sideways and down the windowpane as feelings of rejection and queerness penetrated my soul.

My formative years were not filled with fond memories. In my ideal world, discovering the emotional roads comprising mental maps would have been pleasant and fulfilling. It was difficult to find positive common ground between me and my family members and friends. I also struggled with learning what I was good at. I yearned with all my heart to be the son my parents wanted me to be.

Once, I overheard my father tell my brother, "I wish Jim was more of a man."

Sometimes for a child, who feels different in a myriad of ways, life does not exist as you hoped or wanted.

CHAPTER 8

MAYBE, JUST MAYBE

"Wake up, Jim, wake up. It's time to getta up and going. We've gotta beat the sunrise to getta the bigga catch."

"Dang it, Dad, what time is it?" I rolled over and turned away to go back to sleep.

"It's 3:00 a.m. I let you sleep as long as possible."

I rubbed my eyes, looked at the clock on my nightstand. It showed 2:45 a.m. *Oh my God, what have I gotten myself into? I just want to go back to sleep. I wish my brother didn't have to work today, leaving me to go fishing with Dad.*

Suddenly, a loud crash of thunder shook the house. A huge bolt of lightning lit up an eerie, gray morning sky outside the window next to my bed. *Oh crap, this is just great; it's going to rain.*

"Dad, you always say fish don't bite before and during the rain. Are you sure we should go fishing today?"

"Jimmy, we are going to getta the bigga one today," my dad exclaimed as he headed down the hall to the kitchen.

Darn, he is already dressed and ready to go. No way out of this.

I finally managed to throw myself out of bed and headed to the bathroom before throwing on an old pair of jeans and a white V-neck T-shirt. *How will I ever make it to the car to go back to sleep?*

I stumbled into the kitchen, ready, but not ready, for this fishing trip. Mom carefully prepared an array of food as if we were going on safari. She sang joyfully, showing her happy mood at 3 in the morning.

"Good morning, honey. Are you up and at 'em and ready for a day of fishing with your father? You guys are going to have a great time."

Wow. She's putting two pineapple Danish rolls from the bakery in the cooler for me. She also carefully packed slow-cooked roast beef sandwiches, potato chips, peaches, grapes, Twinkies, tomato juice, dill pickles, cartons of chocolate milk, and several bottles of soda pop. I stood in a daze as she placed the cooler's handle in my hand and gave me a big hug and kiss on the cheek.

Mom turned to walk away, then hesitated and turned back to face me. "This is going to be a special day for you and your father. I feel it. Your dad even told me that on your way home, he's going to stop and buy you a hot fudge sundae. For supper, since you don't like fish, I will make pizza for you and your dad can have the fried channel catfish that you'll catch today."

"You'll get a big one today."

Dad charged through the back door into the kitchen shouting too loudly for such an early hour, "Car is all packed. Time to getta going. Looks like the storm may blow over."

As we backed out of the driveway, I pulled my baseball cap over my face and laid my head between the edge of the front seat and the car window to sleep. It would take an hour to drive to Sassy's hole—a famous fishing lake created by the backwaters of the Missouri River. It required a longer drive than other fishing holes, but Dad always preferred fishing there because he said you never knew what kind or how big of a fish the mighty Missouri river had dumped into this huge reservoir.

The bumps and splashing water from the gravel road ruts off the main highway woke me as we neared the fishing hole. Driving over the top of the dike, Dad began to nudge me back to reality.

"We're here! We beat everyone today and will getta the best spot. The fishes are waiting for us."

The bumps and car ruts of the path leading down to the

water's edge finished waking me. Quiet and stillness engulfed the dark lake. The threat of a storm had quieted the usually noisy crickets and birds. In the distance, subdued flashes of lightning behind some low clouds in a pre-dawn sky were about to give way to a cloudy day. I reluctantly helped Dad unload the trunk. At the lakeside, Dad asked me to open a jar of his famous homemade stink bait and hand him perfectly rounded balls of the bait while he centered a treble hook into each glob.

"Jesus, this stuff really stinks! It smells like rotten cheese. You want me to touch this shit?"

"Don'ta be a baby, son. It's my special cheese bait—guarantee to catcha those sneaky channel catsa. People buy this stuff from me."

I wasn't impressed.

There appeared no way out of this, so I carefully handed balls of bait to Dad, keeping my nose away from the open jar. Dad amazed me when he began to cast the lines with such precision, hitting exact spots he wanted far out into the lake. Each rod and reel was carefully positioned next to each other and in different elevations to catch the beam of the fishing spotlight shining a light out onto the muddy gray water.

Dad placed a plastic tarp on the muddy shore. We squatted down together side by side to watch the lines.

"Isn't this beautiful, Jim? To waits for the light of day and enjoy the peacefulness of early morning. A greata time to justa think about things."

I managed to grunt in agreement. Suddenly, I felt raindrops on my nose and face. Within seconds, the lightning and thunder began, the wind blew. The skies opened with driving rain; the lake filled with "pitchforks."

"Oh shit, here comes the storm," my father shouted. "Come sit in front of me." After I moved, he pulled me closer, grabbing his raincoat and throwing it over both our heads. In a moment that I will never forget, he put his arms around my shoulders to secure the raincoat.

Father said nothing, but his embrace told me what I had

needed to hear for a long time.

Maybe, although I was queer and a sissy, just maybe, my father loved me.

About that time, I looked over to the fishing rod on the far left. "Dad, I think that last rod is slowly moving downward." The movement seemed almost unnoticeable.

"It's notta moving," my father said.

Dad always doubts me, I thought.

"I think it is!" I threw off the raincoat and ran to the fishing rod in the pouring rain. Rain dripped off my cap as I grabbed up the line. The weight on the end of the line felt like a ton of bricks. "My God, Dad. I can hardly lift it."

"Damn it, Jim, the hook and line musta be caught under a log. You will have to just keep pulling itta in. The line will probably break." The line didn't snap as I just kept reeling the log in, walking up and down the water's edge. Suddenly, I saw this huge gray thing in the water.

"I can'ta believe you hauled that huge log all the way in," my father remarked as he attended to the other lines.

"Holy shit, Dad, if that's a fucking log, it sure has big eyes!"

"Whatta the hell," my father screamed as he ran toward me with the fishing net. He tried to capture the huge fish, but the fishing net snapped in two. I kept pulling until my catch landed on the bank. I caught a 23 lb. "buffalo" (a species of fish) on a 30 lb. test line. I had caught a monster fish.

My dad shouted, holding his hands to his head. "This is unbelievable. Whatta good job!" By this time, other fishermen were standing around watching, talking about my expert accomplishment. My father just kept saying, "My son is the besta."

Father bought me that huge hot fudge sundae on the way home. Broke the speed limit all the way. The day had turned out sunny and warm by the time we pulled into our driveway. Dad hung the fish from the roof line of the garage. Mom took pictures until she ran out of flashbulbs. Dad dressed the fish into beautiful steaks to freeze.

The happiest man alive, Dad bragged about me to everyone,

including my brother.

No maybe about it. In his own way, despite our differences, I was his son and he loved me.

CHAPTER 9

FRUIT STAND FURY

"Jim, come here," my mother summoned me on a hot August afternoon. "I need you to run to Harold's fruit stand. Homegrown peaches are finally here!" Standing at the bottom of the steps, Mom opened her clear plastic coin purse and unraveled two, one-dollar bills.

"Oh, your GRIT newspapers came today. You can deliver your GRITs since you have a regular customer down Watson Street on your way to the fruit stand. Remember though, walk fast past that Nita Platter's house. I don't want you talking to her. She's a lady of the night, and I don't trust her! Mind my words, son."

I grabbed a GRIT from the bag sitting atop the old sewing machine in the living room. Mom had just filled it with copies of the paper. I hated selling GRIT, and the bag looked so stupid. It had been designed to open at one end, making it easy to pull out the newspapers. At 14, other kids laughed at me carrying them around. I did love the opportunity to greet older folks who loved the regional magazine-like newspaper from Chicago that was filled with recipes and Midwestern stories. I always took time to chat with my customers. I always related easily to adults, and they liked me. *Why am I so different and like things other kids my age hate?* My favorite stop was the telephone office. The beautiful classy blonde lady there always had two shiny quarters waiting for me—double the price of the paper.

Mom had no idea that Nita was my GRIT customer. I spent a lot of time talking to her on the front steps of her one-room shack made of old brown asphalt shingles hidden behind an antiquated small aluminum trailer. Clotheslines hung with plastic tarp along the front of her property hid her modest home. I had never been inside her abode but could see a simple cleanliness through the screen door and brightly beaded entry.

"Can't talk today, Nita," I smiled and handed her a paper, giving her my usual boyish hug as she held the trailer door open. "Have to get peaches for Mom and get home as quick as I can."

"That's ok, Jimmie. I know you are a busy boy," Nita remarked as she handed me a dime, two nickels, and five pennies for the paper. "You haven't been around much lately, sonny boy. You are finally starting to grow. I think you are going to be a handsome young man real soon."

"Enjoy your GRIT. I'll be down to see you soon," I said, assuring her with another hug and pausing to smell her sweet-smelling perfume before dashing across her yard to the highway. I stood down in the ditch alongside the busy U.S. highway 24 waiting for speeding cars and 16-wheeler semis to pass before grabbing an opportunity to run across to the parking lot in front of the market.

Mr. Harold, a balding, rugged, and time-worn guy, did not present himself as your typical white-shirted grocery store owner. His big brown eyes gave him a puppy dog appearance, but the whiskey bottle hidden under the counter ruled his demeanor.

I walked over to a counter to check out the huge pile of peaches, their sweet summer aroma penetrating the air. Mother had taught me exactly how to squeeze a peach to determine if they were ripe and juicy. The two dollars Mom gave me bought several pounds of peaches and left me with change to spare, so I used the extra money to buy myself a Popsicle.

"Careful crossing the street, little Jimmy," Mr. Harold warned, handing me the brown paper bag of peaches. "Traffic goes fast this time of day. Tell your dad I'll see him Saturday night for poker."

I stepped outside the market in the shade of the old rugged framed store to enjoy my rainbow Popsicle. Mom never questioned the missing nickel or dime which paid for my afternoon treat.

Suddenly, an old Plymouth coupe came speeding off the highway, hitting huge water-logged ruts from the previous day's summer rain. Muddy water splashed in every direction as the car skidded to a stop just feet in front of me. A big, bulky, blond, boyish-looking guy jumped out of the driver's seat, while a tall dark thin guy charged around the back of the car and toward me. Boy, they must be in a hurry to buy cigarettes, I thought. Within a second, the blonde-headed, fat-faced guy in a white T-shirt lunged and grabbed me by my shirt collar and slammed me against the wall of the market.

"You are the sissy GRIT and flower boy that goes to St. Pius, aren't you? You like hanging around old people? You like to suck dick? Fucking little queer."

His buddy grabbed me by my ears and slammed me against the old rusty Orange Crush thermometer hanging next to the entrance of the store. It crashed to the ground. He knocked me against the rough wood shingles and slid my body up the side of the wall. I felt the splintering wood against my dizzying head.

POW. The blonde guy's fist connected with my upper lip and nose. I had never experienced such shock and pain. His grunt magnified the thrust of his fist. The time before each punch, the whole beating, seemed like an eternity. The blue eyes of my aggressor, filled with hate, terrorized me.

Then, with a two-handed downward push, I fell to the ground, my back scraping the wood all the way down to the rocky surface. As they slammed my head from side to side, I looked down to the gravel, feeling warm blood drip from my nose and splatter onto the rocks.

A mean voice ordered the accomplice to spread my legs. The dark-haired guy in his 20's, lodged his feet under my feet. With two big kicks, my legs were spread apart, my crotch exposed. I immediately looked up, hearing that horrible switching sound. The metal of the switchblade glistened with sharpness.

"Let's cut this little bastard's balls off," one of the guys shouted.

My God, where is Mr. Harold or anyone to help me? These guys are going to slice me to pieces!

Pain ravished every inch of my body. I gasped for air from the punches to my stomach, losing touch with reality. My consciousness began to wane as I felt myself drifting into oblivion. Laying on the ground, looking through the legs of the blond guy, I saw Nita on the other side of the highway.

"Leave that boy alone you heathens" Nita screamed while waving her hands. "The police are on their way!"

"Damn, who's that crazy bitch?" one of the guys yelled.

The knife switched shut, and they both headed to the open doors of their car. Then, the dark-haired guy ran back to me and kicked me one more time in the scrotum before running away. I buckled in pain, holding back from throwing up.

"We ought to kill him and you, you stupid bitch," one of the guys shouted. He gave Nita the finger. In an instant, they were gone.

As I slowly eased my hurting back up the wall of the storefront from the ground, I saw Mr. Harold looking out the window above the cash register, shaking his head.

"Please, Mr. Harold, don't tell my dad what happened," I pleaded. "He can't know about me. He would be so ashamed if he knew I got beat up. Please, sir."

"I'm not going to tell Angelo anything. He already has his hands full with you. He's a good man."

Nita waited for me as I limped across the highway. I fell into her arms. Pain overpowered my tears. She helped me to her shack and up the two steps into its modest interior. She laid me down on an old cot next to the door. A few feathers flew up in the air from the pillow. I watched them drift to the floor as my head laid on the pristine, white starched pillowcase.

"I'll get you all fixed up, my dear. Your mom or dad will never know, trust me. Let me help you." Nita's assurance calmed the frenzy in my mind. "You're a special little guy. You don't deserve all your struggles in life. Someday, you will get out of this one-horse town, find yourself, and be a happy man."

"Nita, how can I ever be a happy man when I am queer ... a sissy ... a loser?"

"Do you think you're the only man in the world that likes other men? There are many men and women who like their own kind."

I felt speechless and bewildered for a moment. "Women sometimes like other women? That's not possible."

"Oh, Jim, you have so much to learn. Of course, a woman can want to be with another woman. As long as there is caring and loving emotion, anyone can like anyone...and it's okay. I know how much people teasing and taunting hurts you. Just remember, there're other guys out there like you. You never know, you may even fall in love with a girl someday. It doesn't matter whether you choose to be with a man or a woman. As long as there is love, it's good. Love is all that matters, Jimmie. You have always treated me like a person. Don't ever change from being the wonderful guy you are. Never let other people change you. Never let them cause you to be someone you are not. Now, let's get you cleaned up and home before your mom comes looking."

I left my friend's humble home feeling better physically and, more importantly, better about myself. It didn't matter what my mother said about my friend. She was a special soul in my life.

Mother was so mad about the bruised peaches that she didn't notice my bruises and scrapes.

One day, when home from college, I wanted to tell Nita that she was right. I had found a wonderful girl named Linda and had not forgotten what she had told me. I pulled up to her homestead and emptiness filled my heart when I saw her shack had been demolished and her trailer was gone. She had disappeared from my life, but not from my mind or heart.

CHAPTER 10

116

From early childhood, I had wished to see more than a blur from my 'lazy' left eye so I could have played baseball and football as well as other boys. I also wished to be as smart as the two kids that stood out intellectually during my grade school years. I yearned for the attention and recognition they received from every teacher as the grade level increased from year to year. By the time I reached eighth grade, I accepted being just an average student. Worst of all, I'd decided that I had sexual abnormalities. I would look at other guys and know they didn't think what I did. Once, a ninth-grader flashed his penis in the boys' bathroom, and everyone laughed, but I looked at it in an entirely different way. At an early age, when I watched the introduction to "Gunsmoke" on television, I experienced sexual urges when the main character drew his gun from the holster dangling from his tight pants. My formative years were baffling and filled with mental struggles that were not normal youthful emotions. Lofty goals of accomplishments in school were not always achievable and kept me from using good grades to compensate for my differences.

In the ninth grade, Sister Francis introduced me to algebra, given I made all A's in general math. Within a few weeks, my life began to unravel. No matter how much I tried, I could not do algebra. For Christmas, I asked for a blackboard to hang in our heated back porch and worked for hours diagramming problems, hoping to understand.

One afternoon as I headed out of school to catch the bus, Mom waited for me next to the bicycle rack. When Mom came to town on another day besides Saturday morning, she would walk me a few blocks to downtown and treat me to a hamburger patty and milkshake at the drugstore soda fountain, knowing it would spoil my supper.

"Jim, Sister Francis wants to talk to us," Mom said as we headed back into the school to my classroom.

"James is a wonderful young man, Mrs. Rostello." Sister looked sweetly at me. "He tries so hard in algebra, but something is wrong with his mind when it comes to this subject. I don't have an answer or reason as to why. He does the best he can. I am going to move him back to general math."

As I sat next to my mother, I thought: *This is just great. Now my mom thinks I am not as good as other kids and is embarrassed that I am being pulled from being around the best students.*

In a low, disappointed tone, my mother responded, "Whatever you think best, Sister Francis."

Now my life was flawed in another monumental way. Something was wrong with me, and I didn't know what or why. I knew that other kids with problems like mine just quit school to join the Army or get a factory job. They were often dropouts, thought of as lazy and troublemakers. Fears of inferiority and a destiny of never finishing school turned my world upside-down.

Things began to feel okay after I started making A's again in general math. My learning disability surfaced again in eleventh grade chemistry when I could not solve any equations, use a slide rule, or conduct an experiment outline. I solved that problem by doing any extra credit I could. When my instructor furiously handed me my grade card of a B+, she exclaimed, "You never solved a single chemistry problem. I will never offer extra credit again!"

I faced my chemistry demons again given it was a general education requirement for freshmen at Moberly Junior College.

My high school chemistry teacher had left town, and all my college instructor knew was that I made a B+ in chemistry. I never approached him as I knew he would not believe that someone doing well in all their classes could not perform in his class because of some kind of problem I had with math. I did anything that would help me get at least a C, even if it meant trying to copy off my lab partner, a transfer student recruited to play basketball. He had no correct answers either.

As the chemistry teacher handed me my grade card he heralded, "Good job, Rostello. You got a D-. I hope you're not surprised that I'm not going to give you a good grade just because your mom grooms my poodle."

I knew I had a special problem, but in the 1960s, there was no understanding of my disability. I carefully navigated through college avoiding math. I am probably the only person in the world that graduated magna cum laude from a good college with a D- in college chemistry.

When I entered the public high school (because the Catholic school stopped at the tenth grade), the counselor called me to his office early in the fall. He held his thumb under the number 116 as he placed the results of my IQ test in front of me.

"Jim, your IQ is only 116. Given your IQ, I've enrolled you in co-operative Ed classes and in woodworking and welding. You know, your dad is the best welder in Moberly."

"Is 116 a real bad IQ score, Mr. Mueller?"

"You are barely above average. I don't know how you have made these good grades at St. Pius. It's a tough school. Even with an A- in sophomore English, advanced English and literature classes are not for you. I see you have also requested our new psychology class. This class is for college-bound students. I have made out the best schedule for you, young Rostello."

"What about college, sir? I want to be a teacher, and I'm very interested in psychology. I also thought about being an architect. I love designing houses."

Mr. Mueller sneered as he glanced over my file. "You will have a lot of trouble in college. Being a doctor, lawyer or architect is out of the question. Even teaching would be a rough road for you."

I felt crushed again. First, it was my sexual difference. Now, my dreams to get out of Moberly and start a new life as a good teacher were doused. I hated working on cars and welding with my father.

Embarrassed and dejected, I gazed out the window next to my chair. A beautiful male blue jay attempted to land on an evergreen next to the building. The branch gave way each time he tried to land. Fluttering his majestic wings, he flew up a few feet and landed a bit higher on the branch than before. Finally, the branch supported him. He folded his wings and proudly looked up, down, and around, surveying his new viewpoint on life.

"Are we done here, Jim?" Mr. Mueller asked.

I didn't answer. I picked up the unwanted schedule, then slowly stepped out the door, head down and hopes destroyed. I was a sissy, a weirdo, and now dumb.

As I stepped out the main entrance of MJC with its grand columns, the typical clanking of shutting school doors made me think of that day in May when I left St. Pius X behind. I remember looking back to the window on the second story above the front entrance. Sister Anna Mary peeked at me through the Venetian blinds. Being her favorite student, Sister Anna Mary had loved and protected me. Now my life had left her hands. With a glance back and a smile, I continued on my way in life.

That day as I left MJC, no one watched over me from the window with my best interest at heart. On my own, with my destiny in hand, I walked down the long sidewalk and across the lawn. Reaching the street below the hill, I crossed it and stepped onto the sidewalk along Emerson Street. It would be a long, 12-block walk home.

I suffered agonizing emotional pain as I disappointedly placed one foot in front of another.

Nothing's going right in my life, I thought, stepping onto the curb of a new block. Finally reaching home, I jumped the small creek alongside the gravel road on the side of our house. I sat down on the lawn next to the stream that eventually led down to a ravine a few blocks away.

I thought about happier childhood days when I would launch a stick upstream and watch it snag up along its way but always find a way to get loose and to continue more quickly on its way than before. Suddenly, I remembered the handsome blue jay not giving up until it landed where it wanted.

The stick, the blue jay, and me! I contemplated all those speech contests Sister Anna Mary drove me to, helping me to be the scholar I wanted to be.

"God be with you," were her last words to me.

I crept up the back steps and peered into the house. Mom was busily running the vacuum, unaware I had returned home. I looked down at my schedule of classes again and crumpled it in my fist. *I am tired of my life. I want out of this fucking hick town. I want to design houses or teach school to real children, not cats and dogs. Sister is counting on me to make it in this world. I may be queer, I may be ugly, but I am not stupid. I will make it in college and do what I want to do in life. I am tired of people telling me what to do and calling me names. This schedule is bullshit.*

I turned around and quickly escaped around the back of the house and back onto the street. I raced back the twelve blocks to MJC, arms swinging side to side in determination.

Throwing the door open to the principal's office, I said, "Bonnie, I need to speak to Dean Barnes."

"What's going on, Jim?" Mr. Barnes' secretary asked.

It's time to pull strings, I thought. My mom is a friend of hers. They both work at the Democratic campaign office. Dean Barnes is the father of a good friend of my brother's.

"I need to see Mr. Barnes. My mother told me to talk to you. I need to get my schedule changed."

"Well, have a seat over there, Jim. I will get you into the dean's office when I can."

I sat in a chair next to the entrance of his office. I began to sweat in terror, knowing he had a reputation as a tough principal and did not eagerly cooperate with students.

She finally motioned me to go in.

Dean Barnes looked at me with a strict expression, his black eyebrows clenched below his snowy white hair.

I opened my badly crumpled schedule and laid it on his desk. "Mr. Barnes, I am a good student. I work hard. This schedule is not for me. I want to be a teacher and study psychology. Please change my schedule for me, sir. My parents contributed hard earned money to help build St. Pius and also pay taxes for Moberly schools. Can I please take advanced literature, speech and debate, and psychology?"

Mr. Barnes grabbed my schedule, crossed off shop and Co-op Ed and added the courses I wanted. "Just remember, Jim, I don't want to see you in here in two weeks wanting another schedule change. You better be able to handle these classes."

"Don't worry, sir. You won't see me in here again."

That day launched an important turning point in my life. Psychology and its teacher, Mr. Joseph Williamson, used unconventional strategies. Those strategies changed my life forever and helped me become the person I am today. Although a full understanding of my personal dynamics continued to develop beyond high school, this class became the foundation for my introspection and self-understanding.

Psychology helped me accept my homosexuality. Determining I was not a sinner or evil, I began to understand and not blame others for my choices, to forgive others, and to build pathways in life instead of dead ends.

CHAPTER 11

MR. WILLIAMSON AND MY FATHER

One of my favorite things about winter was the chili con carne served up for school lunches or for suppers at home. Mom's chili was more like tomato juice with meat and beans floating around. Actually, Mom was a superb chef, especially when it came to Italian food.

Today, when I share my cooking secrets to friends they often ask where my ideas come from. Little things like sautéing onions and herbs enough to give them flavor from browning and using tomato paste to get that concentrated marinara sauce tossed with, never poured on, pasta. Putting a small pat of butter at the very end before serving for a more silky texture all came from my mother.

"Mom, why can't you make chili like the school cafeteria? It's thicker and really good, especially now at the junior college."

"Jim, it's the way I do it. You know the leftovers will be thicker tomorrow. You are getting to be quite the chef these days. Dad said you really cooked up a storm when I was in the hospital."

Ah, time for me to give Mom a little lesson on psychology as well as cooking. Mr. Williamson would be proud.

"Well, Mom, guys can be great cooks even though present times may not recognize it. Some of the best cooks in the world are men—" "I know that," Mom interjected.

"It's just a perception that men who cook are sissies. I don't care what society says about it; it's important to me and makes me happy. Mrs. Deeds, my sociology teacher, is on this big 'culture concept' thing, and she's full of shit!"

"Watch your language at the supper table," Mom snapped.

"Anyway, we are not products of our environment though sociologists say that it controls us. This is proven wrong by murderers and people who will not bow down to society. Our 'concept-of-self' is what really matters. Everything we do and how we see it is determined by our conceptual self and trying to satisfy our 'invariant needs.' The true answer is that we interact with our environment and that determines our perceptual-self and then behavior." Looking over the wonderful dinner table, I pointed out: "All I know is that I am a fantastic cook, and the love for it is in my heart, and I feel good when I cook."

Dad started to tear off a piece of Vienna bread as he glanced over at me with a put-off look in response to all of my big talk. But he also liked to hear me talk about things I learned; more so when I was younger and talking about things he understood. I think he began to realize that I would not be taking over the garage business he had built.

"Well, honey, I know what you are saying. You are just being a little more academic," Mom asserted.

Dad began to smile as he knew Mom was my equal and enjoyed when she put my brother and me in our place. He was proud that Mom had also graduated from Moberly Junior College when times were different and harder. She had been one of the most respected bookkeepers in town before she married Dad.

"I will say this," Mom began. "All of us neighborhood gals like to gossip and give advice, but we know in the end people are going to do what they want to do. Take Caroline, for example. Ella and I have told her a thousand times to divorce Billy. He cheats on her like crazy and yet she keeps going back." Mom looked over to my Dad and said, "Did I tell you the other night, in the middle of the night when I got up to pee, I saw Caroline and Billy walk over to the fence between them and Ella. Billy shouted: 'Ella, I'm home now.' Then they both giggled and walked into their house holding hands. You know what that means: she had told Billy what Ella said and now he was getting even!"

Mom continued, "In the end, our opinion doesn't matter when it comes to love between a man and woman. Sometimes it's more than the love of children. Love from that most important person is very powerful. I have learned a long time ago not to get involved in issues between a husband and wife. You will be the loser most of the time. The reality may be that Billy is a no-good louse, but Caroline will see it from her own point of view and her need to have him."

"You are so right, Mom! Our inner-self can even distort things or not see reality. Mr. Williamson has this picture of a woman that when some people look at her, they see a beautiful young woman while other see a nasty witch! Our perceptions are guided by what's inside of us."

"Yes, I know what you are talking about. I saw that same picture in a magazine the other day at the beauty shop. I think it may have been in LIFE or LOOK magazine. The picture was entitled 'Eye of the Beholder' and was very interesting."

My love of spewing my newfound psychological knowledge suddenly brought a problem to mind. Mr. Williamson had put an obstacle in the way of me simply regurgitating the theories he taught us in class. His assignment required every student to come up with a tangible item called a 'mock-up' to demonstrate one of the important fundamentals in his class.

"Well, Mom, now that you understand, listen to this: I have to come up with something that is a hands-on thing that demonstrates a psychological principle and show it in an object. I'm really scared, and I don't know what I'm going to do."

"I can do that!" my father screamed. His eyes glistened with excitement. "When do you need it? We willa build it together. I willa show you how and we'll do it together."

What do I have to lose? I can't do this on my own and my dad can make practically anything.

"Okay, Dad, it's very complicated, but let's try it."

By this time, we were almost finished with dinner. A custard pie was sitting in the middle of the table. Dad helped clear a big spot in front of me on the table and asked Mom to get us some paper and a pencil. Mom moved the pie to the side of the table to let me know it was there when I finished the drawing. Although I loved custard pie, this was my chance to not let my straight A's slip in psychology.

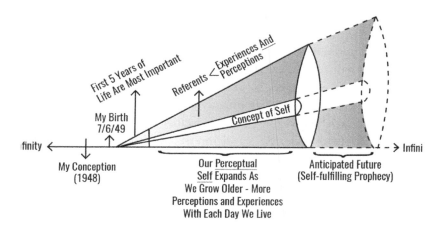

The following Saturday morning, my father shouted down the hall, "Are you woke up Jim? It's already 9 o'clock. I'm ready to work on you thing for school. Getta your clothes on. We willa goes to the truck stop first for your favorite breakfast."

"Warm coconut pie just out of the kitchen and chocolate milk?" I confirmed in excitement.

"That's right! Let's getta going."

When we arrived back from breakfast and went out to the garage, I noticed my father's amazing preparation: heavy steel wire, string-like rope wire, black paint, silver paint, clear plastic, and red-tinted plastic. *Where in the world did he find the red plastic?* He had already made big and little steel framed cones.

"So let's getta going. Explain stuff as we are working so itta come out the way you want."

"Okay, Dad, the first thing we need is a piece of metal going all the way through intersecting the main rod that holds up the cone. There should be some rod before the cone. This shows the passing of time and infinity. Now, right where the cone is going to start, we need a short rod that ends when it hits the cone from the top. This represents conception. You know, Dad, when you and Mom first started my life the nine months before I was born. I am not in the world at this point, but during the time Mom is pregnant, my life is still influenced. If a woman is having problems or doesn't want the baby, it could affect the child. Mr. Williamson even says some new studies show that drinking booze before the birth of a baby can affect the child. Does all this make sense?"

Dad just shrugged his shoulders leaving me to wonder whether he understood. He quickly attached the conception rod to the life timeline with the electric welder.

"Now, Dad, we need a rod intersecting the main rod. This represents my birth and that I have entered the timeline."

Dad quickly severed the main rod in two at the right spot using a cutting torch. Then, he soldered an intersecting rod between the main pipe showing birth perfectly. The work moved so quickly. I could tell Dad had this all planned out. I would hold the rods in place while he masterfully built a perfectly shaped cone within a cone.

"The electric welder is magic," my father asserted. "It lets you build and attach the things while the cutting torch cuts things apart, you see that?"

I nodded in agreement.

"Jim, I think you told me the inner part is most importanté, so we're gonna to use red plastic to wrap the inner frame so it will stand out."

"Cool, Dad. The inner one represents a person's concept-of-self. It determines all our behavior. It attends to, chooses, and processes perceptions and experiences from the environment, represented by all the space between the outer and inner cone. We have the inner cone start out smaller and then get bigger, showing that a baby's life is limited to what the parents provide and quickly changes to all the world as we get older. The inner core is the all-important self-concept. If a person has a positive self-concept, the invariant needs of life are being satisfied, they will handle all experiences within reality. Otherwise, distorted perceptions can lead to non-optimal behavior."

I knew my dad did not comprehend a word I said. But I could see the pride in his expression as I spewed out my knowledge. He tipped his head in smiling agreement to let me know his interest. We were talking man to man, not straight father to sissy son. He respected me.

"What about the metal pieces representing experiences and perceptions?" I questioned. "How are we going to have them floating around in midair inside the cone of life?"

Dad explained as he held up the already stunning mobile, "We'll hang them from the metal braces of the outer edges with thin flexible wires in lots of different lengths. They will be around the middle thing you says is so importanté."

"Wow, Dad. This is really going to look good."

Using the completed mobile, I pointed to help my dad understand. "Dad, what about the end of the inner and outer cones that show 'anticipated future'? How are we going to make them look like the dashes on the drawing? Mr. Williamson says this is the most important aspect of our behavior. The future of our self-concept greatly determines what we perceive and do in life. If we think of ourselves as not worthwhile then we will choose the negative goals and even distort the future. We can actually do things in the present to destroy the future without being consciously aware of it. It's called anticipated future. Mr. Williamson has taught us that what we do today greatly affects tomorrow. Don't you think this is true, Dad?"

"Son, don't mess up our day with talk I no understand. Whatta you do today is all I know about life. Let's just get done what I canna do. So, I am gonna have you paint shiny white dashes on the end of this thing wherever you want to make what you are showing."

Wow, he really has this figured out.

Unexpectedly, my father stopped for a moment as he looked out the old shop window above the cooling trough. "You really like this Mr. Williamson guy, don'ta you? Guessa he is really smart. You wanta to be like him?"

For the first time, I detected a vulnerable side to my father. How do I let him know how much Mr. Williamson means to me without hurting his feelings and that I am glad he is my father?

"He's a good teacher, Dad, just like you are good at what you do and how you provide for us like a good father does." Dad's face glowed with satisfaction.

When we were finished, Father suggested we hang my perceptual cone in my room just above my bed before I took it to school on Monday.

I laid on the bed all afternoon Sunday watching my masterpiece as it slowly turned around and around like a mobile. I realized Mr. Williamson knew best. The object gave meaning to the diagrammed theory on paper. It revealed things about me and my life. I began to understand some answers to questions. Now I knew the answer to Dr. Cain's question, "Why don't you stand up straighter to please your parents?"

I didn't stand up straight because I didn't like myself. I didn't feel good about who I was and I didn't feel equal to other boys. Slouching became my way to live out my self-perception and show my inferior feelings to everyone.

I also began to realize how being different because of my homosexuality had greatly impacted my perceptions and influenced my behavior. Looking at my cone became a mirror to look at and recognize my inner feelings.

Suddenly, my brother poked his head into the bedroom. "Hey shithead, are you going to lay there all day and look at that stupid-ass thing?"

"Probably so, asshole," I proudly retorted.

My perceptual cone would hang indefinitely in the front of the psychology classroom. Other students marveled and were jealous of its perfection. Mr. Williamson continuously praised my accomplishment. The cone I made would be gone from my possession. However, many times in my life, when thinking about myself and the perceptual self, the 'mock-up' on perception helped me understand, accept, and deal with my low self-concept and struggles in life.

I had always wanted a lasting relationship with another man. Often a good person that I liked would come into my life and then would stop seeing me, making me angry. Then, one time, when I told a guy that his leaving broke my heart, he acted surprised and confused. He said my reactions made him feel that I wasn't interested in him and I put him off many times. I realized my low self-concept manifested itself in my behavior. I unconsciously did things to drive him away. Mr. Williamson's "anticipated future" or self-fulfilling prophecy at work. Today, I still don't have a good self-concept, but it's better now to the point that I can accept and live with myself. There is truth in the adage that you must love yourself before you can love someone or they can love you.

The following Monday after building my cone, I observed the bright blue sky dotted with white puffy clouds, looked proudly at my cone as I held it in my lap. I chuckled when seeing a big brown dog galloping up the sidewalk on his way to somewhere important. It was a happy day for me, and I felt glad to be alive, not a common feeling for me.

When we reached my school, I carefully got out of the car with my prize possession. I stood there with the car door open, jiggling it between my thumb and fingers in one hand and the cone in the other. I bent down and looked over to my father.

"I really like my finished project, Dad."

I love you, Dad.

"I think I will get an A."

I love you, Dad.

"Thanks, Dad."

I love you, Dad.

I closed the door. With a smile and a nod, Dad drove away.

CHAPTER 12

MR. WILLIAMSON AND CHERRY VODKA

In looking back at my life from grades one to ten, the rigors of Catholic school helped insulate me from my socially dysfunctional being. The nuns expected intellectual achievement and demanded good behavior. They combined negative re-enforcement ("Jim, you must feel guilty for not being all Jesus wants you to be") and punishment ("James, hold out the palms of your hands and endure the pain of this paddling from God").

My academic prowess and the Catholic environment were the glue in my life. My inability in sports and boy culture chipped away at my self-esteem. I struggled with a self-perception of being ugly, resulting in the bad posture that defined me.

Being dedicated to learning themselves, nuns seemed to value trying to learn all that God has given rather than a high test score. My beloved Sister Anna Mary started taking me to forensic competitions in ninth grade. She never put me down for losing a debate or being terrible at extemporaneous acting. She also wanted to bring notoriety to our school, and she told my mother about a statewide citizenship essay contest that no one was entering. In a rebellious moment, I refused my mother's request to write the essay. But a few weeks later, Sister was thrilled that I had won the contest and we were invited to meet the governor of Missouri in Jefferson City. On the day of the trip, she borrowed the parish station wagon from the rectory and within a few minutes, we were on the narrow 1960s highway with no shoulder going 90 miles an hour. Her veil was flying in the air out of the open window. My mother and I hung onto anything we could. Sister never knew my mother wrote the essay.

Of the many constants of St. Pius, the threads of religious beliefs and consistent interaction of parish families were most important in my survival. Each fall I returned to class members with families that went to Mass with my family. They came from all over the county choosing parochial over public schools. They were like brothers and sisters and accepted one another a little more than in the real world. On a certain level, everyone knew all about each other and even the rich Catholic kids got along and displayed social etiquette. Interestingly, that all changed when we all started public school. Sometimes when Catholic school would begin in the fall, a behaviorally troubled child within a Catholic family would attend, and somehow it all worked out.

During my ninth grade year, Nancy, an eighth grade student expelled from the public high school started attending St. Pius. Her parents, being Catholic allowed her to attend. We started being friends in math class. Although she had anger and behavior issues, it was a chance to have a new friend. We were not the norm and that was our connection. I started hanging around her and her friend Sheryl and a couple of her other friends. All of us would hang out at the drugstore when we could and talk for hours on the phone.

After tenth grade, I started the eleventh grade at the junior college, but had to start the school day for Spanish class at the public high school where Sheryl attended ninth grade. Then it would be a long walk to the junior college for the rest of my day. Sheryl was on the bubble of the in-crowd. Moberly High School's circle of popularity required socio-economic status. This was not like St. Pius.

One day, I was running up the first flight of stairs to get to Spanish class while Sheryl went the other direction to her class. Of course, we were late. As I turned to go up the next flight of stairs, a popular friend of Sheryl's stopped me and said, "Are you for real?" Four vivid little words that haunt me to this day and helped to start me on a path of self-destruction.

The public school world included some teachers who were not like nuns at St. Pius. All nuns through the years knew my class, as a whole, was very poor academically. I sensed they passed that information on to the next Sister. You could see the frustration in their teaching, but nothing was ever said. Amazingly, the rest of my class at the public school was just as "stupid" as my class at St. Pius. My eleventh grade American History teacher one day blurted out, "You are the dumbest class in the history of Moberly." Striving to be a good student, I hated her for that.

I took things and comments too seriously and they manifested a dark side in me.

"Hang up that phone, Jim. I am not going to tell you one more time," Mother shouted from the living room. "What if someone is trying to get a hold of us? You've kept the phone line tied up all night long, it's even too late for me to call your grandmother!"

"Okay, Mom, just a few more minutes. I'm helping Sheryl with her homework," I insisted, trying to get a little more time on the phone. I stretched the old rigid black cord around the corner of the kitchen wall and down the dark hallway to get as much privacy as I could.

"So, let's skip school on Thursday," Sheryl demanded. "It'll be a blast, especially with the cherry vodka we're getting tomorrow night."

"Are you sure we won't get into trouble?"

"Jim, here's how it works. My mom and dad will be at Wednesday night church. Just get out of the house and come over around seven. We'll call a taxi to bring out a pint of cherry vodka. When he gets here, I'll answer the door acting all surprised like I wasn't expecting anyone. When he says he has a delivery for Mr. Daniels, I'll say I don't think he's expecting anything. He will insist that someone called in the order. I'll then say, I'll ask my dad to be sure even though he is in the shower getting ready for bed. I'll walk halfway up the stairs toward the bathroom and shout out to you that a taxi guy is here saying you ordered some cigarettes or something. Your part is to open the bathroom door slightly, staying inside the bathroom, shouting down that you are in the shower, but there's money on the dresser in the bedroom and be sure to give the driver a good tip. I'll go to the bedroom and bring down the money. When the driver sees the tip and knows he will have to take the booze back to the liquor store, he'll go ahead and leave it. Other kids do this all the time, it'll work, trust me."

"Besides that, I swiped some hair bleach and hair color from the drugstore yesterday. I'll bleach the front of your hair while we do my hair. All the 'in' guys look so cool when they do that."

"I'm still scared we'll get caught," I pleaded.

"Don't be such a scaredy-cat. All you have to do is act like you're walking up the steps into school on Thursday until you see your dad drive off, then walk down a couple of blocks to Rollins and 10th Street and I'll meet you there. Mom is at work all day on Thursday. We are going to have the best time. You'd rather have fun than be in school, wouldn't you?"

I wasn't about to be honest and say I didn't want to miss school, especially psychology class. "Hell yes," I insisted. "Count me in."

Mom had grown livid by the time I got off the phone, screaming at me, "Jim, I don't know what I'm going to do about you and these girls. I have told you I don't like Sheryl or Wendy. These two girls spell trouble. I don't like girls that call up boys and talk for hours. I bet you are putting off your homework just because of them, and you've gotten sassy lately. Those two girls have bad reputations. Tell them I don't want them to keep calling here all the time. You better listen to what I say about those two. Do you understand me?"

"Ah, Mom, Sheryl and Wendy are good girls. They try in school. Sheryl is real popular with everyone. I'll tell them I can't talk too much on the phone on school nights, okay?"

"No, son. It's not okay. Either find some better friends or I won't let you continue to talk on the phone at all. And that means to anyone."

"Geez, okay, Mom. It's getting to be like a prison around this house."

Wednesday night went as planned. The cab driver never suspected a thing.

Boy, I bet she's fooled the cab driver a thousand times. She also knows how to steal and lie like a pro. This was a realization that maybe she was not like most of my classmates I looked up to.

I walked into school on Friday morning proud of my bleached hair but feeling guilty about skipping school and worried about what I had missed in my classes. The office secretary and teachers respected me so much they never questioned my absence or suspected Sheryl had called and pretended to be my mom, saying I was sick on Thursday. That made me feel even more remorse. I did enjoy being with Sheryl for the entire day and having a "cool" friend, especially a girl to do girl stuff with and to talk girl talk.

Dad was not happy with my new hair look. "I'd be a Goddamned son of a bitch. Whatta the hell dida you do to yours head? You're fucking crazy. I can'ta figure you out. Boys don't do things to their hair." He continued to swear in Italian. My dad could string curse words together and not use the same one twice more than anyone else on earth.

"Some other boys are doing it these days," I explained.

My dad's eyes popped out of his head as they turned raging blue. "Are you full of shit? If someone jumps into the river, or off of a cliffs, ora licks their own ass like a dog do, are you going to do it too?"

Mom and I knew that the best thing to do at that moment was to shut up. My grandmother on my father's side held her hands over her ears, talking to God while he was cussing in Italian.

Psychology was the last period of the day. I heard that I had missed a good film on phobias. Mr. Williamson, the only teacher with an 8mm and a 16mm projector, showed interesting films. They were all in black and white. As I looked down while taking notes during his lecture, he walked down the aisle to my desk. He leaned over me at my desk. The aroma of his Old Spice aftershave hung in the air. His paisley necktie dangled in my face as he whispered in my ear in a serious tone, "Remain after class, Rostello. You have an assignment to turn in from yesterday."

Wow, this is great! I get to talk to Mr. Williamson after class. Everyone will be jealous that I'm getting special attention.

After the class had left, I gathered up my books and headed quickly to the back of the room. Mr. Williamson had built a cubicle type of office space delineated by waist-high bookcases filled with every book and magazine relating to psychology.

"Have a seat, Mr. Rostello. Are you feeling better today?"

"I think so," I mumbled.

"Okay, cut the bull," Mr. Williamson snapped. "I have some bad news for you. I saw you leaving school yesterday after your father drove away. I have decided not to report you to the principal only because I believe in you and don't want the rest of the faculty to know. It will make them feel disappointed in you like I do at this moment. You understand?"

"Yes, sir. Thank you, sir. I didn't really want to miss your class."

"You know what, Jim? I believe that. Do you know I have big plans for you? I think about you and a couple of my other best students majoring in psychology. I don't want you to lose your way in life. You need to not only learn the principles of psychology but also to put them into practice. You follow what I am saying?"

"I think so, Mr. Williamson."

"Jim, let's talk about the first fundamentals of psychology that you learned in my class. I guess we need to go over them again because it's obvious that you're not using them to understand yourself. They mean nothing if they are just memorized facts. What are the first fundamentals we talked about?"

"The five invariant needs of man, sir."

"Then, I think we should review them right now. What are the first three needs?"

"First is physiological survival," I proudly asserted. "All of us need food, shelter, and other basics for self-preservation. We will fight, steal, or whatever to get what we need to survive. I remember your examples of mothers doing anything to protect their young. Soldiers that do not believe in killing will kill to protect themselves and their country.

"Second is esthetic pleasure and fun in life. All of us need to enjoy a beautiful day, see exciting places, and enjoy pleasurable things that foster a healthy state of mind.

"Third, Mr. Williamson, is the need for creativity. You said that bringing a child into this world is the most creative and beautiful thing two people can do in life. You also said that creating something or doing something like playing music is much more important in building a positive self-concept than passive things like watching TV."

"Well, Mr. Rostello, you have a good command of those first fundamentals of life, and I am proud that you have remembered them just as you have. I'm right about your abilities in psychology. For now, however, we need to talk about the fourth and fifth of man's needs. I think they are more important. What I love about psychology is that it's not just a class or job for me. It's a way that everyone can learn to lead a better life with good choices in behavior. Honestly, I am worried about the fourth and fifth of those needs, recognizing the importance of them, and their effect on making positive choices in your behavior. The fourth need is recognition by those you see as significant. It has a powerful influence on your behavior."

"I guess you mean skipping school when I really didn't want to do it," I confessed, looking at the floor. "I love school and your class especially. It keeps me going. I want to major in psychology and leave this town to go to college and start all over."

"I think you can do that, Jim. I have even told my college professor, who developed the theories that I teach, about you. He is looking forward to you attending Northeast Missouri State if you decide to go there. But let's talk about your recent choices that may be causing you to falter in reaching your goals and staying on the right path in your life."

"Right now, friends your own age can greatly impact you. When you were little, your parents were the most important people in your life; now, friends and society can exert lots of pressure for you to do things to gain their approval. There is the danger that you will lose yourself trying to please them. What I am saying is choose significant people carefully. You follow me? Now, what is the fifth of man's needs, Jim?"

"The need for feeling security," I quickly responded.

"Remember we talked about how feelings of security allow us to make the right choices with confidence and is most important in our lives. Anyone making decisions based on a search for security errs if it's coming from the wrong friends. We achieve security by the first four needs coming together. Feeling accepted by kids your own age is very important and is a source of needed recognition, which, in turn, helps you feel secure, especially during your teen years. Picking friendships with well-adjusted peers who share your goals and values can provide you with the security to do things you should do. I'll say it again, Jim. Choose your friends carefully. Don't sell your parents and other adults short just to be popular with some people. Do you want to be around 'friends' that like to skip school and may have negative personal issues? You get where I'm going with this?"

Mr. Williamson looked straight into my eyes for more than just a moment. As he reached his hand out to me, strong feelings of admiration surged through my mind. I wiped the sweat from the palm of my hand onto my slacks just above the knee. His hand felt so big and powerful as my hand became part of his.

Dad had always told me, "Shake another man's hand with strength. It shows what kind of person you are." That day, I didn't have to try to grip Mr. Williamson's hand. It came as a need inside me to show him that I understood him and now felt secure in making better decisions.

Security allows a little girl hiding behind her mother to look around at a stranger. While holding onto her mom's apron string, she is able to look and smile at him. Similarly, it allows a young boy to climb onto a bicycle with the training wheels gone for the first time. He slips onto the bike while his father's arms hold the two-wheeler firmly as the boy steadies himself. Down the sidewalk they go, the boy pedaling as hard as he can, not scared as his father runs beside him, holding the bike up before letting it go. Then, suddenly, the son rides away on his own, gliding on the wings of his father's security.

I soared the day Mr. Williamson shook my hand. It filled me with feelings of being a good person and that I would be okay. On the surface, things seemed better and that what I had done wasn't out of normal for the teenage years.

To me, Mr. Williamson was the star of Moberly Junior College's faculty. I kinda expected that I would still drink underage and have some social blunders. The Jekyll and Hyde of my troubled personality had not really left; emotionally there was still conflict and low self-identity within me. Looking back, with therapy along with the confidence that Mr. Williamson gave me could have gone deep enough for a real change in my psyche at that time. I was a little too lost in my life, and my weak personality became vulnerable.

CHAPTER 13

HIT THE FLOOR

By the time I reached sixth grade, my introspective ability to entertain myself began to wane. I needed to be around someone besides my parents and my brother. I could see in Mother's face that she knew she and Dad could no longer be all I needed. My brother being six years older was not fulfilling either for him or for me. I did love the few times my brother talked his best friend with a car to take me to a Greyhounds basketball game. Moberly Junior College had an unmatched number of national championships. I loved the players in their silk-like basketball shorts and the cheerleaders.

Jerry was the most popular guy in the sixth grade and picked new friends every few weeks. I figured out that just dropping friends and doing the same things with other kids was his esteem thing. I would see him and his chosen new friends at the drugstore or record store. I would call over and over until his mother would answer and say he wasn't there. He vacillated mostly between me and another classmate, Mike.

Finally, Mike and I started talking and became friends. Soon we were doing a lot of the same things as we did with Jerry as well as our own buddy things. His dad would take us on business trips with him and we both liked academics a lot more than Jerry.

Suddenly, Mike just quit coming to school and communicated

with no one. We could see his duplex row house residence on the edge of downtown from the second-floor window of our sixth-grade classroom. One day Sister Martha had us go over and try and get him to come back to class.

As three or four fellow classmates stood behind us, Jerry and I knocked several times before Mike slowly opened the door standing far enough back to keep more than a normal social distance. "Hey Mike, come back to school. Sister Martha is cool, and we all want you to come back."

"Okay, I'll be there tomorrow," Mike answered, but tomorrow never came.

Out of the blue, Mike came back in the ninth grade. We went right back to being friends and competing for the best grade in biology. This time his troubled dynamics matched up with mine. We created a pad in the dingy basement of his house and our sordid behavior escalated. We would hang dirty pictures, talk nasty about everyone. We started an underground newspaper. In those days, several pieces of carbon paper and pressing hard as we wrote and drew would create five or six pages at a time. He was pretty good at covering sports, and I did geography. Eventually, I would sit in a chair across from him lying on a military bed and we would masturbate.

His mom and dad catered to his violent demands, including getting the family car whenever he wanted. By the time we were in eleventh grade, he was screwing a girl he knew while I just hung out with Nancy and Sheryl. I did hang with Ginny, another friend of Nancy's, that knew the same paper boy that molested me. By then, he was working for the railroad and married. Ginny and I would go their house and play strip poker. I would end up screwing Ginny.

Oral sex started between Mike and me when we were able to get booze. We fought with all our might to get the highest test scores in Mr. Williamson's class. I had found my perfect Jekyll and Hyde buddy.

One evening, Mike picked me up and we headed out to the country to do our thing.

"I couldn't get my brother to get us any booze and I don't think there is anything left at our hiding place." I said disappointingly.

"Fuck," Mike screamed. "My brother is not home right now so we can't call him."

"Well … I am up for some fun anyway," I admitted.

"Damn, I want to get drunk," Mike shouted as he started to drive radically toward the highway. "Goddammit, let's just steal some stuff at that liquor store on the edge of town, the one across from the truck stop. It's all by itself and we can get away with it easily."

I could not believe my ears. I had always feared his temper. "Oh, I don't think we can just walk into a liquor store being obviously underage and pick up something and run."

"Yeah, we can. I heard he sells cigarettes to minors and you could buy some cigarettes and while he is waiting on you, I can come in and act like I'm with you and sneak a pint of something under my jacket."

I was willing to do anything to keep peace and I was mad about my brother for not coming through. *My dad is out blowing money on poker, school is shit, Nancy and Sheryl just use me*, I thought. Truly hating where I was in life, I decided: *Hell, why not?*

Mike let me off at the door and I quickly walked up the aisle to the back counter, "Give me a pack of Kool's" I asked, reaching for my billfold. With a bit of frustration and a what the hell attitude, the owner reached down into the case for the cigarettes.

Mike crashed through the front door. The hanging doorbell rang loudly and shook wildly before falling to the floor. Mike knocked down an entire display of bourbon as he grabbed a bottle and ran out the door. Broken glass shattered everywhere, and the smell of whiskey engulfed the store.

Right away, I could sense the owner knew I was an accomplice. He screamed at me as he reached under the counter. Up came a pistol and he pointed it right at me. "Hit the floor, boy. I am going to shoot. Spread out and get your face on the floor!"

I got between the counter and a display case and dropped to my knees to the dirty brown tile floor. I tried to spread my arms and legs in the aisle but there was not enough room. I maneuvered around with one arm bent on a display case and the other against the counter. I turned my face sideways on the floor to see what the owner was going to do. I crossed my arms, planted them above my head and cried out, "Please, don't shoot, don't shoot."

He grabbed the desk phone and pulled it onto the counter while pointing the gun at me the entire time. "Robbery, robbery, come quick!" he shouted into the phone. He came out from behind the counter and put the gun close to my head. His hands were shaking so hard. I moved my chin to the floor and looked straight ahead when I heard the sirens. Flashing red lights filled the store.

Within a minute, there was a knee in my back and my arms were painfully arched and clutched to my hands. The policeman angrily dug the cuffs into my wrists and locked them. The handcuffs were so tight that sharp pains shot up to my shoulder blades if I even tried to move an inch. The other policeman took a report from the owner.

One of the two policemen drug me to the patrol car and threw me in the back seat just like when I had run away from home many years earlier. Once both officers were in the car, they demanded to know if the guy that came in after me was involved. I was thinking fast and furiously and a corrupt, lying demon rose its head. "I don't know who he was. I saw him parking as I went into the store, but that's all I know."

"Better not lie to us boy, where is your car? How did you get here? Where were you going?"

I quickly explained that I had walked from my house out to see Deborah, a girl from school who worked across the street at the truck stop. She had a car, and I thought we would go riding around after she got off work. She wasn't working so I walked over here from the truck stop to get some cigarettes.

One policeman knew where I lived and demanded me to explain the very long walk from my house to the truck stop. I insisted I had done it before. The cops asked me a couple more things, trying to trap me and get me to the truth. Finally, in frustration, one officer turned to the other and said, "I guess we have to let him go."

From being thrown into the middle of the back seat, I could see a car weaving off the highway and coming toward us. It looked like a drunk had lost control of his car. The headlights were on bright and all of us in the patrol car were blinded as the car got close. The policeman on the passenger side started to brace himself by slamming his hand on the dashboard. The officer in the driver's seat began to maneuver for his gun. Abruptly, the car swerved to the right and stopped with a few feet of the patrol car. Out jumped Mike.

"Officers, officers, I did it. Jim was just helping."

The cop wrestled Mike to the ground and cuffed him. Soon we were both sitting in the police station. The cops called Mike's dad first. He had to take a cab to the station since Mike had been driving the family car. I had never seen Mike's father mad, and he wasn't that night either. He was bewildered and looked scared. He posted bail and then after securing the family car, took me to where my dad was playing poker. Mike and I waited in the car. Then he took me home. I don't know how, but my mother was already standing in the window waiting for us to pull up.

When I entered the house, Mom stepped back from me and covered her face with her hands. Dad raced through the front door. He was as white as a ghost. I sat down on the couch and told the entire story just as it happened. Dad demanded to hear the story a second time. Finally, I slithered to my bedroom and shut the door. Strangely, they sent me to school the next day. They were so mad they hardly spoke during supper that evening. The only sounds were knives and forks clanging, some clearing of throats, and plates being moved around.

Toward the end of supper, the phone rang, and it was our family attorney. As Mom hung up the phone, she told Dad he would have to go to the courtroom in the morning. "Jim might be put in jail." Mom collapsed to the floor crying. Dad never spoke to me the entire two days. To avoid a confrontation, I hardly came out of my room.

The next day my father had me, Mike, and his dad sit in the waiting area outside the courtroom. Within a few minutes, I could see three figures talking to each other through the door's frosted window. The door opened and my father, our attorney, and the liquor store owner came in the room, walked past us, and entered the courtroom door. A short time later, they came out with our attorney and the storeowner left. My dad told Mike and his father they could leave while motioning me to the car.

After we got in the car I asked, "What's going on? What's going to happen to me?"

"I decides to trya save your ass," my father shouted. "I'ma friends with everybody thatta owns a liquor store and they're not so ashamed to know me likes you ares. Harry's droppeda the charges fora me. He saida you seemed differents froma the other kid and didn'ta wanta your life ruined."

Given what happened, the usual screaming and hollering from Dad did not happen. Just looks of shame. Only one punishment: go to confession the next Saturday and Mass on Sunday, and never be around Mike again.

• • •

Being true to the title of my manuscript guided me to tell the story of this chapter. I relive this part of my life every day in shame and wonder about such a dark side of me. Some questions always come up about this memory. Sometimes, it's just a detail like: *Who paid for all the broken bottles of whiskey?* My low esteem and dynamics of my life were dysfunctional.

The plea that I make to all parents is to know that Mike and I were wrong for each other. In rereading my manuscript, I now understand why Mom tried to keep me away from Nancy, Sheryl, their friends, and Mike. My mother knew that certain peers were not right for me. They brought out the insecure side of me. Maybe a parent can share this part of my life when their child questions a parent monitoring their friends. I have never fully understood my behavior back then or forgiven myself for what I did.

CHAPTER 14

TAKE MY GIRLFRIEND HOME

In the 1950s and '60s, my adolescent friends were enjoying their first kisses and interactions with the opposite sex, but there was no one with whom I could share my feelings. School counselors didn't understand homosexuality in those days. You weren't able to discuss homosexuality with anyone. Friends, relatives, and priests never talked about it and wouldn't have even admitted to knowing a homosexual. My brother's group of friends even beat up a guy because they heard that he had given some other guy a blowjob.

My father—the best welder in Moberly, known and liked by everyone for his outgoing, Italian personality—could never deal with the truth about me. This became evident when he would question me about my friendship with girls.

One day, Dad called me out to the backyard. With one hand in his pocket and the other holding a cigarette, he asked me about Sheryl.

"Dida you lets Sheryl dance withs another guy? Go outside and talks to him and lets her leave with him? Darrell trusted only you to take hisa daughter ons a date, and then yous let hera do that? What'sa wrongs with you?" Dad stared down at the cigarette in his hand and didn't make eye contact with me or wait for me to respond.

My perception was that he didn't want to hear a single word. He walked back into the house, puffing on his cigarette and mumbling to himself in Italian, which he knew I didn't understand. Later, I found out from Sheryl that her father had said that I was either "a Goddamn pimp or a fucking queer," but my dad didn't hit him.

I walked over to the dog pen. Our two hunting dogs, Picca and Brownie, were eagerly waiting for me to pet them as they pushed their noses through the fence. Picca's name came from the Italian word piccoli, which means "little one." Dad loved her small size and acute intelligence, but both dogs had so much love to give. When things were wrong, they would listen. With their butts shaking and light brown eyes looking up at me, I confessed to Brownie and Picca, "I'm a homosexual. Do you still love me?"

I knew in my heart I could always count on their unconditional love.

CHAPTER 15

MY FIRST KISS

During my mid and late teens, I had become an overachiever in school and a workaholic when not drowning myself in my studies. My differences left me somewhat socially isolated and dependent on myself to not be bored with life—to find some sort of happiness. Earning and saving money allowed me to gain a sense of control and distracted me from feeling my unacceptable attraction to guys. Money would be my ticket out of Moberly and having it depended on me since both my parents had become ill by the time I entered the ninth grade.

My mother was one of the first women in Moberly to have open heart surgery at the University of Missouri Medical Center in Columbia, just thirty-five miles away. Rheumatic fever as a child had destroyed her mitral heart valve. At only 15, I demanded to see my mom immediately after she made it to the recovery room. Walking up to my mother's bed, seeing her beyond-pale face, unconsciousness, and bags with tubes everywhere, undermined my promise to hold back my tears and be strong. Lightheadedness, dizziness, and a numbness in my legs were the last things I remembered before crashing to the floor.

Coming up with the $2,500 for the surgery nearly bankrupted our family. No welfare or financial assistance existed in those days, and my father was not working. My skill in the kitchen allowed me to feel I contributed in some small way by fixing meals for my dad and brother. In the 1980s, my mother had two more heart surgeries. The surgeries were successful, but unscreened blood resulted in her getting hepatitis C, which plagued her for many years.

My father nearly died four times from major heart attacks, three of them in front of me as a young boy. During the attacks, I would run to a place in the house where I could see him, but he could not see me. His face would turn purple as he clutched a chair or table, bending over in excruciating pain. The onset of loud belching would signal the worst might be over. Experiencing my parents' illnesses removed me from the happy-go-lucky life as a young teenager. I vividly remember my father feeling responsible for our money problems. He missed his work and the things he loved to do. Anger and bitterness accelerated each time he tried to return to work only to have another attack.

Life with my dad grew ever more unbearable. Making money by taking any job available seemed the only way to have the things I wanted and to afford college. The popular kids in town with the influential parents landed the good jobs. Grocery bagging jobs at the Kroger supermarket downtown were given to the cute and popular jocks.

My family dynamics would provide me with a job opening. Dad seldom drove Mom downtown for shopping. He would say, "Your mother canna go inna store and twenty people will go in after her and come back out before she does." Mom relied on cab service, leading to my first "real" job. The woman who owned the Yellow Cab Company in town thought I was cute. She loved me calling her beautiful though she wore too much make-up. I always loved to compliment people and say nice things that they never heard from others.

When I turned sixteen, she offered me a late night and early morning dispatching job at the cab station that included being a Western Union operator. It all sounded so exciting. I worked full-time during the summer and Saturday nights during the school year. As soon as some kids at school found out, they teased and ridiculed me calling me "cabbie." But I had money in my pocket to solace me. With it, I was able to buy a bleeding madras suit jacket that all the "in-crowd" guys wore. Obsession with having money emerged as the addictive pill I depended upon to get rid of unhappiness and insecurity.

The cab office was located across from the train depot in the roughest part of town. The old and dilapidated building had been built in the 1800s. The linoleum had worn down to the wood floors. The waiting sofas and chairs were dirty, torn, and smelled old. The bathroom in the back had an ancient type of commode that I had never seen before with a toilet bowl black with grunge.

During winter, the large floor-to-ceiling windows allowed the cold wind to chill me to the bone despite a small old-fashioned electric heater under my office desk. Sometimes when the drivers were on a call, I became afraid to be alone after midnight. With four or five bars within the same block, things could get very unpredictable in the waiting room. I would hide at my desk behind the old oak Western Union cubicle style counter, which had a protective glass shield along the top and a small customer window.

Larry, a handsome wild man, regularly came in on Saturday nights. He would stumble in drunk with a different "lady of the night" every weekend. His good looks always got my attention. Sometimes I would raise my head enough to sneak a look at them making out, hiding just under the Western Union logo beveled in the glass. Watching the woman run her fingers through his coal black hair as she kissed him passionately made me want to be her.

Damn, Jim, it's okay to jack off with some of your friends. But, thinking about kissing this guy? This just isn't right. Kissing is for people in love, and you can't love another guy. That's wrong. Damn it, I don't want to feel this way, especially towards him. He's just a rounder and probably has syphilis and every other disease under the sun.

Late one Saturday night, Larry floundered into the lobby, stumbling, and grabbing onto the edge of the service window to steady himself.

"1205 Ault Street," he demanded, staring at me with his deep brown eyes.

"I'll have you a cab in just a minute," I promised. "My driver is on his way back from a run right now."

Larry staggered over to an armchair to sit down. He slouched down, allowing his arms and hands to flop on the armrests.

He's probably going to pass out, I thought before getting back to my game of solitaire.

Suddenly, he began to rub his crotch on me. I hadn't even realized he had slipped around the counter to the side of my chair. *What in the hell is he doing?* He grabbed me around my shoulders, pulling my body toward him by rolling my old, wooden swivel chair toward him as he grabbed my crotch. He drew close to kiss me. My reflexes propelled me out of the chair forcing my back against the wall. He tripped over the leg of the chair as he attacked me, giving me time to run out of the cubicle to the back room.

I slammed the door to the back behind me and grabbed for the old skeleton key dangling from the lock. It fell to the floor. I bent down and grabbed it as quickly as I could to lock the door. I jiggled the key to no avail. "Lock, damn it. Lock … lock!" It finally engaged and I turned the key, securing the door. I threw my back against the door and held onto the knob so he couldn't turn it.

Pounding the top of the door with his fists and kicking the bottom, he shouted, "I'm going to fuck you boy!"

I began to tremble at the thought of him forcing himself on me and hurting me.

What if the driver comes back right now and saves me, but sees this? What if the driver tells my parents?

Suddenly the Western Union teletype began chiming and I could hear the tape spewing out of the machine. *Oh, my God. What do I do now? I can't miss a money order that might be coming in, I'll be fired.*

I put my ear to the door. I couldn't hear anything on the other side. *God, I hope he's gone.* I threw open the door and ran to the teletype machine. Larry had disappeared. I quickly acknowledged the incoming message and then ran to the front door to lock it. Looking out the all-glass door, I saw Larry talking to the cab driver. Thank goodness, he's paying for his fare ... *Oh, thank you Lord, they're getting into the taxi to leave. It's all okay now, no one will ever know that you have been part of a man-to-man sexual attack.*

I charged back to my desk to get everything back in order before my replacement arrived. I figured the cab driver would pick him up after taking Larry home. My relief dispatcher finally walked into the office. The cab drivers were required to pick up and take home the dispatchers that worked the graveyard shift. I walked out to the cab, parked on the side of the building and started to get in the front seat to get my ride home.

"Don't sit up front," the driver ordered. "I have to pick up 925 Concannon Street on the way and take him to work. He likes to sit in the front seat and talk."

I jumped into the back of the car. Being alone in the dark backseat actually sounded good. I didn't want to talk to anyone.

No sooner than I shut the back door on the passenger side, the driver side back door flew open and in jumped Larry. I quickly grabbed onto the back of the front seat, begging the driver to help me. He was already peering in the rearview mirror. Larry lunged toward me, pinning me down in the back seat by straddling my legs with his. I felt his erection against my body. He grabbed my arms and held them behind my back.

His mouth smelled of beer and smoke. He overpowered me, forcing my lips open. His tongue sank deep into my mouth. I gagged, feeling his spit slide down my throat. In a burst of rejection, I pulled myself loose and turned my head against the seat so my attacker could not continue to kiss me.

"Stop this car! Stop this car! If you don't stop this car, I'm gonna jump out," I screamed.

The driver finally stopped halfway down the block and I vaulted out, tripping and falling against a parking meter as I focused on the alley a few buildings away. Reaching the alley, I began to run wildly to escape.

After looking back to see that no one followed me, I stopped to push two garbage cans apart, giving myself a place to hide. I squatted down, balancing myself on my feet and bracing my back against an old brick wall. Garbage juice oozed out of the bottom of a trash can and ran between my feet. My shoes stuck to the asphalt. The smell of garbage began to turn my stomach, making me gag and vomit. I put my hand around my nose to stop the smell and rose to my feet to run.

The predawn air hovered thick and heavy, with a Midwestern morning fog engulfing the dimly lit alley. I began to run all the way home, which was at least two miles from downtown. I ran as fast as I could, stopping only when out of breath to bend over and grab my knees to gasp for air before continuing on.

What possessed the supposedly straight cab driver to set me up by getting me in the back seat and then waiting for Larry to get in the car? Did everyone in Moberly know I was queer? Think I would let a good-looking guy rape me? I carried guilt my entire life for that initial attraction to a guy who had tried to rape me.

Neither the cab driver nor Larry said anything the next time I saw them, and neither did I. That's the way my first kiss by a man had to remain.

CHAPTER 16

THE LOTTERY

It's ironic in life: no matter how much we sometimes wait or want for change, when it finally happens, we hang on to the past.

At 20, the time had come to leave for my junior and senior years in college. I stood at the bottom of the concrete front steps of our homey brick bungalow looking up to the empty, second story window nestled in the gable. By getting away from 1128 Emerson Street, which harbored the troubled yet bittersweet years of my life in Moberly, I could begin my own personal journey.

Dad opened the worn, stained front door, and stepped out onto the porch. "Mom is right behind me, Jim. We're ready to leave."

I stood on the driveway, peering at the brick chimney which triggered many happy memories of beautiful fires expertly built by Dad in the living room fireplace on winter nights. These were brief moments that made him happy, and for me, eased the difficult times.

Looking down the side of the house, I caught a glimpse of the dog pen. Brownie and Picca squeezed their noses through the fence to gaze down the driveway at me. Their brown eyes twinkled in the sun as they squirmed, beckoning me.

"Wait a minute," I shouted to my father. "I'll be ready to go in just a second, there is something I need to do. I need a few minutes alone with the dogs."

Discarding my old, leather soft-sided suitcase alongside the stately front evergreen tree, I bolted down the driveway to the dogs that summoned me. Brownie, the old mama dog, forced her nose further through the fence as I approached. Slobber dripped from her long, extended tongue as she tried to lick me when I reached for her. Picca moved back, letting Brownie gain my attention. I grabbed the top of the metal rail with one hand while reaching the other through an opening to pet my soulmates. Leaving the good times of my life behind with my true buddies became much harder than I imagined.

"I'm going to miss you guys." My voice broke. "You've been my friends through all my struggles with Dad and with life in this miserable town. Brownie, you are getting older now, girl. I may not be here when you leave for dog heaven, so let me say my goodbye now, just in case. Picca, you take care of your mom. Hunt lots of quail so we can have quail and polenta when I'm home again. Love you both, and I'll never forget you. I promise. Your love is in my heart. Being without you will be hard no matter where life takes me."

I pressed the palm of my hand first onto Brownie's brown and white head. Then, I patted Picca's orangey-brown colored nose. After taking a few steps away, I turned back for one last smile to my friends. Then it dawned on me: those dogs loved me even though it was my father and brother that took them hunting. I walked toward the car where Mom and Dad were already waiting in the front seat. The sun dried the tears in my eyes.

It was time to go off to my new beginnings in life. Dad had already put my bags in the car. As I started to get into the back seat, with my hand on the car door handle, memories compelled me to look up the street. Eyeing the corner, I thought of the many times I trekked to the grocery store for Mom. The neighborhood bully who had repeatedly beaten me up no longer threatened me. Moberly had continued to change as well as me. Whether good or bad, this town would always be home.

My brother had gone to Northeast Missouri State College. I decided to attend this college, too, since that is where Mr. Williamson had gone. His professor had big expectations for me.

Driving the 65 miles to Kirksville, Missouri, I relived many childhood memories. Familiar landmarks along the highway faded in and out of my thoughts of what the coming days, weeks, and months would bring. This time, each passing farmstead, creek, or valley heralded my new life. The shackles of the past were gone, the promise of tomorrow raced through my mind with dreams of a better life.

As we turned off the main highway and headed down the street to Dobson Hall, my new home, I looked at the backs of mom's and dad's heads as they stared out the car window, not saying a word. Their silence told me their thoughts on my leaving.

"Mom and Dad, I am going to miss you. I know I may not get home every weekend or month, but trust me, I will do you proud. Okay?"

Mother turned to me and smiled as she wiped away tears from between her eyes and glasses with her fingers.

"My dear, dear son, I know you've been waiting to get out of Moberly. I know more about you than you may realize. You're a fine son. I know it's your time to live. Letting you go is part of what a good mom must do."

Dad grabbed the top of the steering wheel with one hand, reached his arm across the back seat pointing at me. "You better getta home lots to see your mother, boy. You know your mom is notta doing good from her last heart surgery and you better notta forget your responsibilities to be there for her. We won'ta be around forever."

My father did not mention his most recent of his heart attacks or whether he cared if I came home to see him. *Why did my thoughts and actions always have to be about what he needed or wanted me to be?* I knew his time on earth was limited, but with new goals swirling in my mind, that edict had lost its power.

"You want to see me too, right, Dad?"

"Don't worry about me, son. Do right by your mom and

remember where your home is."

Life was better at college even though I remained in the closet. My relationship with guys hinged on the facade that guys were to look at, but never touch. I still had never come to know any college friends who were living a gay lifestyle in small towns of northeast Missouri.

A wonderful new friend named Dan came into my life. He worked as the mail room clerk. Each day as I got to know him better, I became more and more sexually and emotionally attracted to this friendly guy from just across the Iowa/Missouri border. His smile matched his personality. Hearing him say, "How is my buddy, Giuseppe? Nothing in your mail slot today. Maybe I should write to you," brightened my days.

He always had a smile, and his sexy blue eyes twinkled as he chatted. I had begun to understand and identify those that might also be gay or at least open-minded, though it was not okay to chance saying or doing the wrong thing. Dan's masculinity and attentiveness to me, more than to any other man, brought sunshine to each day. I knew he knew that I checked the mail each day without really expecting letters from home. I found our friendship fulfilling even without sexual dimensions. Although the physical attraction became intense, neither of us were willing to risk stepping out of the closet.

I had begun to build friendships with many guys on my floor in Dobson Hall. My self-esteem grew with each new friend and being accepted as a normal person changed so many feelings in me for the better. My lack of athletic ability, and enjoyment of cooking and ice skating were no longer issues in my life. However, the community showers in the dorm confirmed my attraction to men. It allowed me sneak previews to a life I had yet to experience. Every time I turned to rinse gave me a chance to enjoy a man's body.

One day, Mrs. Rath, the dorm's widowed housemother, came to my room to hush the loud friends visiting me. "You and your friends need to keep it down up here," she demanded in a stern, but motherly, fashion.

As she peered into my room, I looked across the hall to the open door of my neighbor's room. He unzipped his pants behind her back and, with a smile, pulled out his "Mr. Nasty" and shook it at her. Although I enjoyed the sight, being treated like one of the guys emerged as the most important thing. Maybe I am not gay or a sissy. Other guys were not afraid to be "guys" around me. I had started to become happier.

Then, on December 1, 1969, a traumatic event would intensify the realization of how much I cared for men. The Vietnam War grew more intense each passing day. President Johnson and Congress had implemented a lottery to determine draftees. As the day of the lottery drew close, every young man became more scared of how it would affect them.

When it came to luck, I could hold 499 lottery tickets out of 500 and still lose the draw! Good old Rostello luck. The evening of the lottery, groups of guys gathered in rooms where someone owned a TV to watch as their fate was drawn out of a hopper. Each capsule had a date on it and the order of the dates would be the order guys would be drafted. If your birth date appeared in the first 100 capsules drawn, you were destined to go to war or defect to Canada. I knew I would never make it in Vietnam. *God, please help me this one time.*

Although he had a darling girlfriend who lived across the street in the girls' dorm, red-haired Bill, a sweet and cute new buddy of mine, always included me. The lottery official had called Bill's birth date: April 26th, number 59. The announcement brought a look of shock, terror, and bewildered sadness to his usually happy-go-lucky expression. Guys drawing the early birth dates headed out to find booze and get drunk to help them get through the horrible news.

During the drawing, I began to wonder if I had missed the calling of July 6th. Unlucky me, surely, I could not have a safe number. *When is my day going to be called?* The announcer then called my birth date on capsule number 318, which meant that I would be among the last to go to Vietnam. I stepped out in the hall and fell to my knees and thanked God.

An important prologue to my life would unfold that night. Bill got crazy drunk and showed up at my room at about two in the morning. Having classes the next day didn't matter. College would soon be ending for him.

"Can I come in for a while?" Bill pleaded.

"You bet you can. I am so sorry for you, Bill. It's going to be alright. I believe it in my heart. This war could be over tomorrow before you're ever called."

Bill came into my room and flopped on my bed. I sat in my desk chair next to the bed and tried to make some small talk. My roommate, also having the bad news of a low number, stayed out all night with his friends. Before Bill passed out, he turned in my direction and reached out to me.

"What will happen to me, to my life? I'm so scared Jim. My cousin is already in Vietnam and writes home with such horror stories. He sleeps on a bunk sitting on open slats a foot or so above the ground. Snakes crawl on the ground just inches below him. Kids come up to American soldiers carrying bombs. They have to cut and spray weeds just to protect Americans."

I reached over and took his hand. He held so tightly to my grip as I patted him on the shoulder. Then, in an instant, he passed out holding on to my hand. In all of his pain and his need for comfort, I realized how much being there for another man meant to me. I knew that being gay meant something more than sex. I sat up for hours just watching him sleep until he finally let go of my hand and turned over. I slept face down on my desk.

When I awoke a few hours later, Bill had disappeared. I wondered if he remembered anything about coming to my room frightened and needing the closeness of a male friend. For days, I could close my eyes and relive how tightly he hung on to my hand.

Bill and his girlfriend never returned to college after Christmas break. I heard from his roommate that his draft status notice arrived a few days after New Year's. I wanted to write or call him, but that was just not a straight thing to do in those days. For the rest of my life, hearing the name Bill or seeing a guy with brownish red hair and brilliant white teeth igniting an infectious smile, I would think of his sweet, unrehearsed personality.

One evening a few years later, I sat in a campus pizza joint. As the people left the table in front of me, I noticed a young man sitting alone. His unbelievable similarity to Bill drew my attention to him. Even after we looked into each other's eyes, he did not look away. The moments became surreal, and my mind drifted to thoughts of my friendship with Bill and the bonding that took place on the night of the lottery.

Is that Bill? I knew it wasn't, yet my heart and soul wanted it to be him.

Bill proposed to his girlfriend and planned a wedding upon his return from Vietnam.

I believed Bill would be a good soldier.

CHAPTER 17

CONFUSION AND DENIAL

The first Friday night back to college as a senior was a happy time in my life. The Moberly-Huntsville Musketeers always gathered together in the dorm room of our self-proclaimed leader.

With a twinkle in his eyes, John smiled. "Tomorrow night is the freshman dance at Centennial Hall. Just think, all those cute freshman girls finally away from their homes and looking for hot older guys. The pickin' will be easy."

"What about Debby?" Guy interjected.

"It's an unwritten custom that it's okay to pick up a little 'strange' before you get hitched," John asserted.

We all agreed to crash the freshman dance the following night. Doing guy things with straight guys stopped the haunting of my Moberly past. As we took turns sipping Jack Daniels from our half-pints during the dance, my glance caught the rich brown eyes of a cute girl standing alone after her friend began to dance with someone else. Her hairstyle, somewhat old-fashioned, captured an innocence in her eyes and smile. She possessed subtle yet phenomenal beauty.

I maneuvered around the room ending up close to her to stage our meeting as coincidental. I called it "the Rostello shuffle."

"Hi, would you like to dance? Jim here."

"I'd love to. I'm Linda."

I took her hand and led her to the side of the dancing crowd. As we began to dance, I instantly knew this really nice-looking girl had not been spoiled by popularity in high school or family money. She was from a small town in Missouri only about fifty miles from Moberly, which gave us geographical common ground. Talking to each other came easily. We set our first date for the next night.

The next few months emerged as a unique time in my life. Linda changed with each passing week, letting her hair grow long and straight. She began to wear more makeup, showing off her beauty. My buddies would comment, "You lucky dog. She is good looking. How did you get her?"

Soon Linda and I were steadily dating and spending many hours with other couples late at night, sitting staggered up the stairs. All the couples made out on the semi-circled balcony. There I discovered that love had been born between us and that I could enjoy an emotional as well as a physical relationship with a girl.

Like the perennial weeds that had been removed from a well-kept garden, my confused feelings would sprout again. Many times, as I kissed Linda under her earlobes, I would look behind her back and catch glimpses of other guys and girls making out.

Is it really normal to like watching guys make-out with their girlfriends? Jim, you fool, it's not right to be wishing to be the receiver of the lovemaking by hot guys. But you do get sexually aroused with Linda and love having her in your life. Are you being fair to her?

Seeing Dan every day at my dorm became really bothersome, reminding me of my attraction to guys. I desired to be with him and struggled with loving two people at once in different ways and for contrasting reasons.

My mind would soon be invaded by another shot of guilt and a reality check. One member of our buddy group never really gained acceptance because of his constant bragging and conceit. One night, John had enough. After Melvin had left, our leader announced, "It's time to teach Melvin a lesson. We'll use the infamous circle jerk. I think Mr. Know-It-All is a fruit anyway. This will put him in his place, letting everyone know he is not the man he thinks he is."

John began to lay out the plan, sensing from our expressions that some of us had no idea of what would take place.

"We're going to take Melvin for a little drive in the country. I'll challenge the manhood of the group by the traditional bet of each guy throwing five dollars on the ground in the middle of the group. We'll be standing next to each other in the darkness. We'll tell Melvin that the first person to shoot will announce themselves as the winner. Then, each of us will pretend to yank out our dicks and jerk off. Of course, none of us will be doing anything. We'll use our hands to hide that we are not really jerking off. Leave the rest to me."

I doubted anyone's willingness to participate. No one but John really thought this plan would work.

The next evening, John suggested getting some booze and driving in the country. Although Melvin became apprehensive upon hearing about the circle jerk challenge, his bluff had been called. We finally reached the place staked out by John: a rutted gravel road alongside a cornfield. We all formed a circle and threw our bets in the middle. It was pitch black and easy to pretend that we had all begun to jerk off.

Within a few minutes, Melvin began to shout out his victory.

By this time, John had stepped back to his truck and flipped on the truck lights at just the right moment.

"You fuckers," Melvin screamed falling to his knees to hide his erection. In a moment I will never forget, he looked directly at me.

He knew I would have liked to do this with guys.

He knew by the way I stared at him that I loved his well-hung body.

He knew I had betrayed someone that was like me.

Melvin avoided the group after that night. Often, when passing his dorm room, I thought about knocking on his door and telling him my regrets. The following summer, Melvin drowned while swimming in an old mine quarry. I carry regret and shame to this day.

The crabgrass of self-doubt about my sexual identity had begun to invade my mind. Questioning the honesty of my relationship with Linda, I stopped calling her and just wanted to be alone. Dan could not even cheer me up with his blue eyes and smile. I resented him for creating my unacceptable feelings.

One day, after handing the clerk some change for gum at the student union candy counter, I turned around to face Linda waiting right behind me.

"Jim, why haven't you called me? What happened? Did you find someone else?" She asked, her eyes downcast.

"Linda, I just needed some time. Seeing you now, I know I want to be with you. Just been busy with my classes."

"I want to be with you, too," Linda whispered. Her genuine affirmation opened the door in my mind to forget Dan.

At that moment, I began to deny my homosexual feelings and behavior. I would look away from attractive guys as much as possible. I never let myself be around Dan much, concentrating on guy things like my bowling team, and telling myself that I could handle a heterosexual life with Linda.

CHAPTER 18

SACRAMENTO

The longer Linda and I were together, the more my confusion about liking guys instead of girls faded into total denial. Our activities with straight college couples became fulfilling and fun. Linda, school, bowling, and partying brought a joy that I had never known growing up in Moberly. When we visited my parents, Dad loved to tease Linda. He thought she was so good looking. His face glowed when he heard that my independent bowling team beat all the fraternity teams to win first place in the college league, telling Mom and Albert, "My boy finally did okay in a sport."

Luckily, I did enjoy my heterosexual relationship to the point that repressing sexual interest in guys became easier. I lived in a world that worked. Linda had small-town values, so the sexual aspects of our lives were not important. French kissing and going no further than panty play sufficed.

My junior and senior years passed quickly and student teaching time arrived. I returned to Moberly so that I could live at home and save money. Being a large high school, Moberly had a larger curriculum that allowed me to teach my beloved geography. By this time Moberly had built a new, four-year high school. Mr. Williamson remained at the Junior College, so I could not student teach under him.

Linda wrote to me every day. Mother happily gave me the letters and encouraged me to sit down and write back right away. I knew she hoped we would marry, that my life would be normal, and she would get the grandchildren she wanted. My brother and sister-in-law did not plan to have a family.

My co-operating teacher loved me. My supervising teacher from Kirksville would exclaim, "You're the best student teacher I've ever seen." He was tall and handsome, creating that little detour in my mind. I wanted to be good at teaching for him as much as I did for myself and Linda. This strange motivation tugged at the walls of my denial.

"Finding a large high school to teach geography and psychology will be difficult," my supervising teacher warned. "I'll do all I can to help you find the perfect high school."

Mom expressed more worry about me leaving Moberly than whether I would teach my favorite subjects.

I said, "Don't worry, Mom. I'll find something and at least stay in Missouri. Millersburg has a sixth-grade opening, but I don't want to teach elementary, I would almost rather work at the bowling alley."

About a week later, while mowing the backyard, Dad came up to me and said, "Go inside and putta on a clean shirt. We're gonna go for a ride. Don'ta question me, just do as I says."

"What's the deal with Dad?" I asked passing Mom in the kitchen on the way to my bedroom.

Mom quickly looked away. "Just go with your father and try to keep an open mind."

Within moments, we were headed down the highway toward Millersburg, though I had no idea that was the destination. In those days, two-lane highways still went through the business district of even small towns. Millersburg's downtown included a two-story, red brick building on each corner, featuring a bank, drugstore, and a grocery market. Like most small Missouri towns, it had died on a state highway. Commuting from Moberly would be my only chance for a life.

The minute we turned at the stop sign and I could see the

school; I knew my fate.

"Stand uppa straight, Jimmie Joe. Say whatever the boss of the school wants to hear. You know whatta to do. You're the college guy."

The superintendent waited in front of the old brick school built in the 1920s. While talking to some locals, he shouted at us as we pulled up and stopped, "Hey, Angelo, my hay baler has run perfect since you fixed it, it's not missing a bale. Looks like there's lots of quail this year. Come and get 'em. You're the only one I let hunt on my property." They walked ahead of me into the school and his office. Once inside he handed me a stack of books, including math, science, English, and, of course, boring history.

"I've already contacted Kirksville," the superintendent announced. "They'll give you a temporary elementary teaching certificate if you go to summer school. Here's your contract."

It all happened so quickly and there wasn't time to make the decision that it was the job I wanted. I guess it wasn't my choice to make. As we were leaving his office, the superintendent slapped another blow to me. "Your father says you have a chauffeur's license from your work as a taxi driver back in Moberly to get through school. I have an opening for a bus driver. It's a long route that leaves at 5:30 in the morning. Let me know if you want it."

Oh my God, one of the drawbacks to teaching is getting up early. And now I'll have to get up at 4:30 am!

My enthusiasm for teaching melted into disappointment. Returning to college, I attended a required group discussion about our student teaching experiences. After the meeting, Dr. Evans, my supervising teacher, handed me a note with a name and phone number on it.

"Jim, there's an opening at a brand new consolidated high school east of here, near Hannibal. It's for geography and psychology! I just knew this would happen for you. I already talked to the superintendent at Highland High School. Call him immediately and the position is yours."

I could barely contain my emotions, and I didn't dare tell Dr. Evans I had signed at Millersburg. My elation quickly dissipated as I thought about how to get out of that job and not be disowned by my father. My appointment would be in just two weeks when the new superintendent would be filling all positions at the new school; I had to think fast.

When I got home to Moberly. My mom was so elated at the thought I would be home to stay and commute to Millersburg. Dad said he had been looking for a good deal on a car for me to drive every day to work but hadn't found one yet. I couldn't wait any longer for my own car to sneak to the interview that Dr. Evans had set up. He had told the Highland superintendent that I was the best of his student teachers and a top graduate.

How do I get Dad to even consider driving me to another job interview?

"Dad, would you drive me to a high school near Hannibal. There is a teaching job there that my supervising teacher told me to interview with. I'm worried if I don't do it, it may hurt my grades with him when I start my master's degree."

"Hell, we better do it then. I'll drive you."

Highland High School turned out to be everything I wanted. Several young teachers were at the same interview for other teaching positions. The principal promised to be strict. I would teach my double majors, geography and psychology, the very subjects I wanted to teach. The superintendent offered me a contract, wanting me to sign it immediately. I explained that I had signed for an elementary job thinking I would never find a high school psychology position. The superintendent assured me that if there were any problems getting out of the Millersburg contract, he would work it out for me. That's all I needed to hear. I walked out of the interview with a signed contract in my back pocket. I got into the car feeling happy and scared at the same time.

Dad never said anything when I got into the car or questioned me about the job. Instead, he just seemed in a good mood. "Since we are over this way, you wanna stops along the Mississippi anda do a little fishing? There's a good spot justa on the other side of Hannibal. I already told Mom we mighta stop there. I threwa some old clothes in the trunk."

"Do we have to? I have some stuff on my mind."

"Okay, we'll justa stop in Hannibal for a fresh catfish meal."

"Dad, you know I hate catfish."

"Yeah, you'd rather eat all that other crap like that fried 'skrimp'. You canna order whatever you want."

I gotta tell him the truth. The longer I wait, the madder he'll be. Oh God, help me. I know what I'll do. I'll pull out the teaching contract and tell him when we approach the double yellow no-passing lines at the top of the next hill. These fucking, narrow two-lane highways are so dangerous.

Damn, here comes a big hill—wouldn't you know it.

Just as we began to crest the hill, I pulled the teaching contract from my back pocket and began to open it.

"Dad, I need to tell you some—"

"What'sa that paper in your hands Jim?"

"Dad, I signed a contr—"

"Thatta yellow paper looks like the thing you signed at Mil—"

"Dad, I took the job at Hi—"

"Did you sign something backa there?"

"Dad, try and under—"

"You fucking idiot! You agreed to work somewhere else after you give your word to someones else?"

"Please, please, let me expl—"

"Sacramento!"

Oh my God, Dad said Sacramento, the worst Italian cuss word. I am in so much trouble.

My father slammed on the brakes sending the car into a skid and onto the gravel shoulder and started to fishtail off into a ravine. Letting the steering wheel go and then grabbing it several times, Dad got the car to fly out of the descent and we emerged back on the highway heading the opposite direction back toward Highland. I could not believe what had just happened. I broke out in a cold sweat.

"You're gonna to march yourselfa back into thatta school, you little shit, and give backa the job. You understand me? Don'ta you knows whatta giving your word to someone means?"

"Dad, please try and understand. I want to teach what I want to teach—to high school kids, not babies. And what about Linda. This school is only 35 miles from Kirksville, not 80 miles like Millersburg. I can see Linda every weekend, and if we get married, I can even commute with some other teachers that live in Kirksville."

Dad didn't say anything. He just kept driving toward Highland.

What am I going to do?

We pulled into the circle drive in front of the school. Dad drove toward the entrance of the school, but when we reached the school he turned the car away and headed back out the other side of the circle drive. I didn't know what was going to happen. We pulled out onto the highway and headed toward home.

"I give up on you. You're stubborn, justa like your mother. I don'ta understand you and don'ta think I ever will. Let me tella you, I'm notta afraid. I woulda make you take the Millersburg job, butta your mother will just give me so mucha hell, it's not worth it. It's over. I will take care of getting you out of the Millersburg job. Justa don't talk anymore. Do whatta you want; you always do what you want. Justa remember, I'ma not going to be around mucha longer, and you'd better takes care of your mom when I'ma gone."

Dad died from his fifth heart attack one year and one month later.

CHAPTER 19

THE ENGAGEMENT RING

Life grew happier each day during the summer of '71. At 21, I had landed the best teaching job, started to work on my master's degree, and bought a car of my own. I drove to Kirksville to bowl and see Linda. I always enjoyed bowling with good women bowlers; the best woman bowler asked me to join her team. My bowling excelled to new levels. I averaged 180, a good average in those days, and I bowled a 270 game.

Shrouded in love and security, my relationship with Linda evolved and solidified. Happiness and relief are wonderful emotions to feel at the same time. Repressing the attraction to guys soothed my mind. The gratification and social approval of possibly choosing a straight life had sequestered my homosexuality. I became so happy, I would often sing to myself while driving in my car, "Oh what a 'beautyful' morning, oh what a 'beautyful' day, I've got a 'beautyful' feeling everything's going my way."

One Friday night, a friend approached me during bowling.

"Hey, Jim, Peggy and I are going to her mom's tomorrow for the weekend. You and Linda can stay in our trailer." He winked and smiled.

Wow, finally the right place for Linda and me to go all the way! This will be a big step in my life with Linda.

The next night, Linda and I snuggled together in bed. I used the same foreplay I had with wild Cindy during my high school days.

Wow, Linda's new panties are embroidered, I thought, making each move carefully and slowly. I wished men's underwear had been more exciting in those days. When the timing became right, I eased my hand lower and lower. I halted at the right moment and slipped off my briefs with one hand while keeping the other in place. Easing myself onto Linda, I kissed her from her neck and down into her warm cleavage.

"Oh Jim, feeling that part of you on me scares me. My virginity worries me. I've always wanted to wait until my wedding night with you. Is that okay, honey?"

"Yes, sweetheart. You know what? Let's go to your parents' house next Friday night and tell your parents we are getting married and then to my parents' on Saturday after we stop at a jewelry store in Moberly."

"Oh, yes, Jim. I'm so happy."

"Linda, there's one thing. My parents will ask if we are getting married in the Catholic church. Are you okay with that?"

"Yes, that's alright. I belonged to a nondenominational church at home, and I've enjoyed going to Mass with you now and then."

Wow, everything is turning out perfect.

We held each other close and fell asleep holding each other.

Everything turned out great during my first year of teaching and being engaged to Linda gave me the future I'd always wanted. I took Linda to the high school homecoming parade and dance at Highland. I had formed a psychology club with my students, and we had built a float for the homecoming parade. My students loved me and were eager to meet Linda. When I was in high school, my dad would not let me drive the family car, nor would he drive me on a date to homecoming dances, so I missed going to them. Now, even that void in my earlier years was laid to rest.

One member of my psychology club, Tommy, attended the homecoming dance by himself. He embraced his homosexuality, holding true to himself even in those days. He swished around like a weeping willow on a windy day and amazed everyone on the dance floor with his acrobatic dance moves. I could tell it grated on Linda's nerves.

"That kid is a real femme," Linda announced in disgust. "Why does he act that way?"

"He's a good student and a nice kid," I said, defending him. "It's kinda cool he's not afraid to be himself."

"Baloney," Linda sneered. "You think his behavior is okay? Boy, you'd better not let my oldest brother hear you say that."

My thoughts began to swirl in fear and uncertainty. A new nail had lodged itself in my mind. An irreconcilable distance between Linda and me had emerged. Being like Tommy could be very easy for me, I admitted to myself. With all the good things that had happened in my life, I still realized my behavior was considered abnormal and dared not admit to being different. The most courageous thing I could muster regarding Tommy, "Oh, Linda, he will grow out of it someday and be a normal guy."

I had no doubt, Linda had begun to change. My encouragement to let her hair grow longer enhanced her good looks. She began to room with a popular girl in the dorm and run around with her friends, propelling her popularity on campus. Linda's in-vogue dialogue and assessment of others led to feelings of dismay in me. She would call anyone she didn't like, or thought uncool, a "retard." Finally, one day I carefully suggested that it was not a very kind term and didn't show an understanding of the mentally retarded or the field of psychology.

"Things are changing for the mentally retarded," I asserted. "They deserve to be and will someday be treated like everyone else in this world, no longer locked up and hidden out of sight in their homes. There is even a facility to be run by the college called a Learning Center opening next year. And, Linda, you may not believe it, but they know when they are called names, and they feel pain."

"Oh, good grief," Linda snapped. "It's just a joke. You've been teaching too much psychology."

I relented, saying nothing more.

As the August wedding date grew closer, it became time to

start attending marriage counseling with the priest; a requirement for a non-Catholic person to be married in the church. We picked the young, cool priest for our guidance sessions.

He and Linda are sure "hitting it off," I observed as the counseling sessions moved forward. Something about him emerged that I began to dislike. During one session, Father Neil speculated that Linda and I didn't communicate effectively because we never argued or fought with each other.

"That's just not my style," I insisted. "Besides that, Linda and I are happy and never have had a reason to fight. For me, my mom and dad did enough of that to last me a lifetime."

"Well, I'm going to bring two Styrofoam bats to our next session. I want the two of you to role-play a disagreement and hit each other with the bats until you are both mad and get everything out. This will foster communication between you and improve your relationship. It's a new form of therapy. Jim, I'm sure you know about it from your training in psychology. I think Linda is okay with it."

Are you fucking kidding me? What is this kook talking about? This is absolutely crazy. What does he know about us? If he weren't a priest, I'd tell him off right now.

"Father, please forgive me, but I just can't hit Linda with a Styrofoam bat. It'll hurt her at least a little bit. Guys shouldn't hit their girlfriends. This is too strange for me … hmmm, I guess we can let her hit me if you want. It'll give her practice for hitting me with a real bat after we're married." I laughed out loud as I slapped my hand on my knee.

I soon realized that Linda and the priest were not laughing at my joke. Linda just sat quietly; her hands folded in her lap. I reached over and put my hands over her wrists, then, lovingly slipped my fingers between her fingers.

"Is it okay if Linda and I talk about this, Father?"

He didn't respond. Linda never mentioned it after we left the session. Neither did I. The whole thing seemed so ridiculous to me that I never gave it any merit. I was glad when Father did not show up with Styrofoam bats at our next meeting.

Linda and I planned to live in the housing for married students after our wedding in August. She would finish her senior year in Kirksville, and I would carpool with other teachers who were also teaching at Highland. Many had spouses still in college. Not being home to see my parents all summer, Linda suggested I go home the week of July 6th to spend my birthday with my parents, which seemed strange, but I just guessed she would probably come to Moberly the day of my birthday. I loved birthday surprises.

Bowling ended about 9 pm on the Friday night I planned to go home, so I took Linda to her dorm right after bowling to get on the road. When we got to her dorm, Linda told me to pull around back and park so we could talk. I loved our chats and holding each other in the front seat of my car. That evening had been a good bowling night. I looked forward to holding Linda and relishing my scores.

"Jim, I've decided we should not get married. It's nothing you've done, it's just me. All my mother ever did with her life centered on raising my four brothers and me. I have been meeting with Father Neil and he—"

"You've been meeting with the priest without me? I don't think that was right ... ahh, so you've been talking about me all this time. It all makes sense now, you knew about the Styrofoam bat role-playing, didn't you? So, he's been raising doubts about us in your mind?"

"Jim, he gave me this book called Johnathan Livingston Seagull. It's a little book about this seagull, different from all the others. He wanted to fly a little higher and do different things with his life. I want a different life from my mother's. I don't regret our time together. I'd like to keep the engagement ring if that's alright."

"Wait a minute. You're going to break up with me because of a fucking seagull? None of this makes sense. You're finishing college. Your mother never did that. I don't want a jillion kids—you can have a career that most women don't have if you want to."

"Please try and understand that us being together is just not right for me," Linda admitted.

"Oh Linda, this is just marriage jitters. Everything will be okay, I promise."

"I don't want to see you after tonight, Jim. Do you understand? Please don't try and see me again."

"No, I don't understand and never will. There has to be a reason. Something more than just an existential book you read. Please tell me ... is there someone else?"

"No, there's no one else. Please just accept my decision. Promise me you'll go straight home and drive careful and take care of yourself."

"I feel like just driving off a bridge, Linda. This is all so sudden! I can't believe this is happening. I'll go if it's what you want. Keep the ring."

After she got out of the car, I watched her walk into the dorm and out of my life. So many things tormented me during my drive home. I wanted to die. *What would my life be without Linda? I have lost everything. How will life go on? Dad will have been in bed for a long time by the time I get home. He always goes to bed as early as the chickens. Mom will be surprised but will be able to handle it. I've got to tell her first and let her talk to Dad. She'll stand by me.*

Mom was reading her Reader's Digest and watching the late show as I entered the front door. "So glad you're home honey, I always worry about your driving so late at night—my God, son. What's wrong with you? You look like you've just seen a ghost." She jumped up and ran to the window to see if my car was there.

I dropped my laundry bag of dirty clothes that I had brought back from school on the floor and sat down on the arm of the sofa. Mom always did laundry for me when I came home. "Mom, Linda broke up with me tonight."

"Oh, nonsense. You all just had a fight. What did you do to her?"

"Nothing. Mom. Honest. She just wants a life without me."

"Well, you've got your work cut out for you. You better get her back. Work things out. I don't know what to say to you right now. You'd better get to bed and think about what you have let happen. We'll talk about this in the morning." Mom walked to the front door and let the dog in from his last duty of the day. I knelt down to welcome him. He stopped to lick me on the face and headed to the bedroom with Mom.

No sooner had I crashed into bed than the light came on in Mom's and Dad's bedroom. *Oh, my God, Mom never wakes Dad up after he's gone to bed, not even when Albert or I have come home too late at night and she can smell booze on us. I wonder what they're saying in Italian.*

Suddenly, I heard Dad cussing. "I'll be Goddamned. I'll be Goddamned!" Then, he shouted down the hall to me, "We wantta know whatta happened—why you anda Linda broke-up?"

"I already told Mom, I didn't do anything. Please, I just want to close my eyes and sleep. Just leave me alone for tonight," I yelled back.

"The hell we will," Mom screamed. "You've got explaining to do. This is no time to think about yourself. What are we going to tell the grandparents and everyone down on the farm? There has to be a reason. Spill the beans!"

Dad must have said at least a dozen times, "I'll be Goddamned. He'sa fucked things uppa again."

"Dad, I didn't do anything. Things aren't always my fault you know."

"Did she give you back the ring? If she didn't, that's a good sign," Mom concluded in a rampage of questions and thoughts.

"She wants to keep the ring, but she made it clear she doesn't want to see me again. That's all I know."

"Angelo, I'm not getting any answers out of Jim. I want you to drive me to Kirksville tomorrow. I'll find out what happened from Linda and while I'm at it, I'll get the ring back."

Oh my God, I've lost Linda and now I'll be the laughingstock of Kirksville.

"I'ma not driving to Kirksville anda facing thatta girl. Fuck thatta shit," my dad screamed.

"You're my husband. How much do I ever ask from you? You are either with me or against me on this," my mother argued.

"I'ma notta going to letta him have us do hisa dirty work,"

Dad insisted. "I'da rather go in his room righta now and makes him tell us whatta happened … no talk, no sleep and then in the mornings make hima drive to Kirksville and getta the ring back."

"Oh, Mom and Dad, please just leave me alone. I can't take anymore tonight. If you don't get off my case, I'm leaving right now and driving back to Highland. I don't care what time it is. Please, please, I don't know if I'll be able to make it there."

"Leave. Go ahead and leave if you want. We don't care about you or what you do."

I can't take this any longer. I ran to the front door crying, "I'm leaving, I'm leaving."

"Go, go," my parents shouted in unison. I gathered my belongings and started to leave. Opening the door halfway, I put my suitcase out on the porch, then reached back in the house to grab my duffle bag. I saw our French poodle, running to me. He had his red squeaky ball in his mouth and dropped it next to my foot. He sat down, his big, black eyes looking at me. Then, he spoke to me: Jim, be strong and leave. Make it back to Hannibal. You need to be alone and sort all of this out. I love you. Throw me the ball before you leave.

I looked into the eyes of our dog, picked up the rest of my things, and headed out the door. I didn't throw the red ball for him.

I threw my stuff in the car and sat in the front seat looking at our house.

Surely Mother will come after me and talk me back inside.

Instead, the lights in their bedroom went out and the house became dark. I cringed, sitting in disbelief.

"No, she's not coming. My mother has turned on me, her own son!" I shouted to myself.

Finally, I backed out of the driveway and pulled my car about 50 feet in front of our big garage next to the house. Out of sight, I slammed my head against the center of the steering wheel, pounding my fist on the dashboard. The absolute worst feeling in the world, wanting to cry and yet not able to, took control of me. I could hardly breathe.

My God, I want to die.

I finally got myself together. It was a wonderful feeling of relief when a solution to all my problems came to mind. *Damn it, I'll do just what I told Linda I would do. I will drive off a bridge somewhere between here and Highland.*

I threw the car into first gear and peeled out onto Emerson Street—I was on a mission. The determination and courage needed to drive or jump off a bridge boggled my mind.

The pain of Linda leaving me and my mother's abandonment gave me no choice but to kill myself. My solution would be to get even with them. Besides that, I didn't want to live any longer with my uncontrollable feelings toward guys. Lying to the world and to myself constantly pestered me.

The first bridge, about five miles north of Moberly, didn't seem to be the right place. From being there to hide some booze for parties in my younger days, I knew it was not dangerous enough and too close to home. Reaching Macon, I thought about the train viaduct on the edge of town, but that would be messy. Jumping into darkness would be easier. Just north of Macon, I decided on the bridge that appeared the largest and about my only choice. I pulled the car off the highway a bit past the bridge and began to walk back to check out the spot. A car zoomed past, then another, both sounding their horns letting me know I was walking too close to the road. *Damn, there are a lot of cars out for two a.m.*

I stood at the edge of the bridge, looking down into the darkness below. My life is as black and forbidding as this. I scooped a few rocks with the side of my shoe, big ones and little ones, and kicked them off the cliff into the ravine and creek. Immediately the loud chirping of the locusts ceased. Stillness seized the night. *Those bugs are afraid to let anyone know where they are just like I'm afraid to let anyone know who I am. They may have to live like that, I don't want to. Damn, here comes a big truck.*

The loud blaring tooting horn of the semi-truck warned me of my dangerous location, too close to a spot on the highway with no shoulder. The wind shear of the passing truck forced me to take a step back. Instantly, I began to slide and lose my balance. As I grabbed for the side of the bridge trestle, my feet slipped out from under me. My hand could not reach around the large outer bar. I kept grabbing with all my energy. Within a second, my other hand grasped an inner trestle allowing me to pull myself up and onto the concrete foundation of the bridge. Relief filled my mind and soul. I broke out in a cold sweat.

Oh God, Jim, you're okay. Jesus, I almost fell to my death. Damn, Jim, you do want to live. You don't want to die. God has given you a second chance. I'm really like those locusts that choose to hide in order to survive. I don't have the balls to kill myself. I want to live, even if it means being alone in this world and living a life hidden from others.

My relationship with the universe that night became more spiritual than religious.

Quickly running back to my car, I began to cry uncontrollably. The relief of choosing to live and accepting my life allowed me to live with the pain of being unloved. I noticed a narrow gravel road and drove down the road leading to the ravine and creek below the bridge. The fading sound of the highway traffic soon brought comfort and aloneness. I began to pray.

God, oh my God, thank you for being with me tonight. Maybe you really do love me regardless of what the world wants and tells me to be. You understand me and have always been there for me, and I know that your love is unconditional for as long as I choose to live. I am sorry I tried to kill myself tonight, knowing that is the most mortal of sins. Please forgive me and help me.

The hot long night began to give way to misty morning dew. I got out of the car to pee. Walking down the road to the creek, I began to think through my life. *Jim, you're a good person even though you are different from most everyone you know. Being different doesn't mean you are wrong. You're a good teacher; your students love you. If you have to live in this world alone, you can do it. There are people who care about you. Aren't you glad Mr. Williamson didn't have to hear that you killed yourself instead of relying on the principles of good living he taught you? Remember when he told you that everyone must love themselves first, that although we all need the significant others in our life, we cannot let them distort our perceptions of self and dictate our thoughts and behavior? I understand now, really understand what you were saying. I just hope my students get from me the same wisdom I got from him. Damn it, I do like guys. Maybe Linda is not for me.*

Maybe real happiness is down the road for me by being with a guy. Jim, you know you want that more. It's time to stop worrying about Linda and Mom and Dad, or anyone. You've always wanted to go to California. Even Kansas City or St. Louis is better than this hell hole. I am not going to let anyone control my life. No one is worth destroying myself over. I'm going to get out of this part of Missouri.

I marched back to my car with a newfound confidence and peace. Driving back up onto the highway, I could see the first glimpse of morning's pale colors on the horizon. The dawn grew brighter quickly. The longest night in my life finally relented, but I still spent many years being afraid to tell people who I was until things changed in this country.

My relationship with my mother forever changed the night I left home after the breakup with Linda. My mother had really never empathized with struggles and difficult times in my life.

After my breakup with Linda, I remained her son and she continued to be loving on the surface and generous to me. She never questioned me about not bringing home any girlfriends. I just can't describe in words the way things became different, not good or bad. I kept my distance from my mother until she died.

I remember vividly the first night of her wake. I looked down at her with my back to all of the mourning friends she had made among the senior citizens. The only thing I could think about was the night she became so angry and abandoned me over my broken engagement. I had forgiven her many times, but during the funeral, I could not keep from thinking about the past. I accepted that Linda had been brave and courageous enough to be true to herself, but I couldn't forget the way my father and mother let me leave that night.

It's strange. I have had many ups and downs with friends and lovers in my life. Sometimes relationships and friendships were severed over something I could not forgive at the time. Now, many years later, I couldn't accept what happened between us.

The memory of my mother and our relationship tormented me at the time of her death and while writing these memoirs. Over the years, I continued to relive this part of my life over and over. The more we love someone, the easier it is to forgive, yet the harder it is to forget.

CHAPTER 20

PROMISES, REALIZATIONS, LIFE CHANGES

The morning after Linda and I broke up, I finally arrived at my apartment near Highland High School. Sitting in my car, I looked across a field of clover to a brick, Cape Cod style home that I had loved since first seeing it. Though my rural teaching job only paid $6,800 per year, I had dreamed of owning that home with Linda and our children someday. With that part of my life gone, the decision to explore my feelings toward men now weighed heavy on my mind. Loving my teaching job and all the wonderful parents, students, and other teachers threatened to derail my determination to leave Missouri.

The first few surreal weeks without Linda created a void in every moment of my days and nights. As time passed, students, parents and other teachers had heard the small-town gossip of my broken engagement. They stopped by to offer encouragement and friendship. I knew they were right in reassuring me that time would heal my heart, but I didn't want to hear it.

Rural town school districts can be quite different from city schools. Parents had me over for dinners, fellow teachers and students dropped by to chat and everyone wanted to help.

Leaving Highland would mean surrendering the last important relationships in my life. My students loved me. Other teachers deeply respected my rapport with students. I had formed a psychology club with my prodigies entering studies and experiments in regional and state science fairs—unconventional in those days. Psychology was a subject some considered non-scientific. The sense of family outside the classroom enriched my life as well.

Like my students, teachers were genuine and loving. Many of them farmed along with teaching. The Mississippi sustained and enriched life. I never tired of crossing the mighty river on an old, two-lane highway bridge, contemplating all it gave to big cities, small towns, and its nourishment to farms and wilderness from its spring floods.

Vince, a favorite teacher friend, knew the river and its secret fishing holes and rich hunting hideaways. My favorite gift from "Ole Mighty Miss" were wonderful delicate morel mushrooms, never raised outside of their natural environment at that time. Elusive as anything in nature, their wild woody flavor and the challenge of finding them thrilled me in springtime. Their sponge-like structure was camouflaged among the previous fall leaves, making finding morels both difficult and rewarding. Vince and I hunted for these mushrooms in mid-spring when the May apples were out. I could never find these reclusive treasures on my own. Breaded and fried was the only way to enjoy their flavor. My teaching buddy knew where to look and let me keep all that we found together.

One day while knocking down brush with sturdy tree branches as we forged through the woods, Vince shouted, "Stop right where you are, Jim. Don't take another step."

I immediately thought I had stumbled onto a snake in my path.

"Look down at your feet," my scout shouted.

To my amazement, I saw morel mushrooms all around me and looking in all directions ahead of me, morel after morel came into sight. An entire grocery sack full.

My mentor patted me on the shoulder as he looked at my overflowing bounty. "Morels are kinda like life, Jim. What you want can be all around you, and yet you don't see it. A hard-learned truth, don't you think?"

As the weeks passed, time did begin to heal the pain of lost love. I still cried alone at night or when thinking about what might have been. My breakup with Linda had happened in early summer, so severing my teaching contract was not an option for that year. I also needed the love and support of the people around me.

Highland had been good to me. Even the coaches and jocks were my friends. I couldn't understand why I always bonded with jocks and coaches. We had such great times. I felt like a different Jim Rostello than the boy who'd been so terrible at sports while growing up. They protected me, wanted me around, joked with me, and were my close buddies. Silly interactions, like who would get the shortest haircut, entertained students and staff. Life had improved in many ways since I had left Moberly. Though my breakup with Linda had tainted my college years, they had also been great because of good friendships, soaring academic success, and bowling. My three years at Highland nurtured a yearning to be a true guy.

Homosexuality never ceased to raise its ugly head. Randy, an assistant football coach, lived in the apartment next door to me at Lewistown, near Highland. Handsome and muscular, he hooked up with women from Hannibal and Quincy. They would play all night at his apartment next to mine. I could not resist listening to their sexual talk and thinking about her giving it to him. It made me feel ashamed and confirmed my feelings of abnormality. One morning, I joked privately to Randy. "Boy, Randy, you were sure having a wild time last night. The banging against the wall and all the grunts kept me up all night."

"Yeah, this gal had such big tits. It drove me crazy, and I screwed her all night non-stop. Sorry we kept you up. Guess I owe you one. Tell you what, why don't you come over Thursday night, and we'll both bang her."

Excitement began to swell in my mind and body. "Sounds great to me," I admitted.

The revelation that haunted me after the night with them centered on the lust of watching him with her and then going where he had been. His role excited me more than my time with her.

Somehow my students always figured out things and nothing got past them. Several of the kids in my classes commented about me getting back to my old self. They encouraged me to ask out a newly hired teacher in the building.

"Sandy is really cute, Mr. Rostello."

"She's after you, Mr. Rostello ... we can tell she likes you."

"When are you going to ask her out?"

My students could talk me into anything. In my mind, going out with Sandy proved that I had put Linda in my past though she would never know it.

One Friday, Sandy invited me over for dinner, detouring my promise to not date women. The lights were low, dinner included locally butchered steaks with a joint offered as dessert later in the evening. Then she suggested going to the bedroom. Linda never wanted to give up her virginity, but Sandy was the very opposite. She desired it all night long, which is not something a fake heterosexual wants. I left in the middle of the night, thankful to have successfully gone through the motions so there would be no gossip at school. I broke up with her the following week.

My students pumped me for information even though the word circulated that I had spent the night in Hannibal. My classes were happy about that, seems like they always noticed when my car was not parked in front of my apartment.

Though Elizabeth was my favorite student and president of my psych club, I liked all my students, especially a co-captain of the football team. He loved my psych and geography classes. A handsome jock, his dad was an influential person in the community. At age 17, he looked more mature than me at 23.

One night, he showed up at my place alone. Usually, he had his girlfriend, Becky, with him. We would talk about their future, school, and life away from a small town.

"What's up, Mr. Rostello?" Brian asked as he opened the storm door, jingling his car keys in his hands.

"Not much. Just grading some papers and going to watch 'The Waltons' pretty soon."

"Becky and I just had a fight. She wants me to go to college where she is going, and her rich parents have it all planned out. But I don't know if she is the one."

Against my better judgment, I let him in. Brian talked about breaking up with Becky and going to a college with a good football program. Her not-so-perfect reputation also seemed to bother him. I followed him to the door after talking it out. He seemed like he had made some decisions.

"Guess you really helped me tonight, Mr. R." As we reached the door, he grabbed my neck with his hands and teased, "I guess I won't have to prove to you that I can whip you at wrestling."

"Think what you want, you whippersnapper," I joked.

Suddenly he grabbed me around my chest and wrestled me to the floor, pinning my legs under his knees. Then he spread my arms and held them down with his hands.

"See, I gotcha, teach." Sex and excitement filled his raging blue eyes. When his crotch brushed mine, it confirmed my perception.

I turned my face away from him focusing on the baseboard across the room. "Brian, let go of me now. Leave. Leave right now. Don't say anything. Forget this and don't come here alone again."

Brian's hands swiped my face as he pulled away to let go. I shook and shuddered as I watched him leave. I never let myself be alone with him again, for his good and mine. Homosexuality had been all around me all my life, like the hiding morels. I didn't want to see it.

One day while diligently checking out teaching positions listed at the Registrar's office in Kirksville, I noticed an opening for a teaching job in the small town of Wellsville, Kansas, not far from Kansas City. I knew that no matter how much I loved Highland, my life would be better by moving to the bright lights of a big city. It would be teaching a class called "The Me Nobody Knows," which would replace the traditional citizenship course. I interviewed, got the job, and moved the following summer. Mom, still trying to cope with the death of my father the previous summer, created some guilt. But I kept my promise to do what seemed best for me.

CHAPTER 21

A BABY CHRISTIAN

It took me a lifetime to learn we create our own disappointments by unilaterally embracing expectations of people and places. Wellsville, a small town thirty miles southwest of Kansas City, beckoned me with a new start in my life and closed the window on my past. I planned to teach my favorite classes again, meet new parents that cared and students that were typically ornery yet genuine. I found that none of that happened. All small towns and its people are not the same. Whether the proximity to a big city or changing values in the 1970s, the joy of teaching vanished. I felt unable to establish student and teacher rapport. Each morning I laid in bed as long as time would allow to avoid crossing the street to start the day. Negative feelings plagued my life.

I found Wellsville much different from my upbringing in Moberly and my first years of teaching at Highland. Wellsville's negative attitudes toward teachers, their values, and lack of respect for traditional social graces were a shock. My first year as a teacher attending the graduation of my students said it all.

As I sat among the other teachers on the gymnasium floor, all dressed-up and proud, in came the parents in jeans, halter tops, and cowboy boots. "My God, some of the boots those parents are wearing could kill cockroaches in the corner of a room," I exclaimed.

The classy female teacher sitting next to me said, "Welcome to hick suburbia."

Then, came the 'hooting' and 'hollering' when each of their little darlings' names were called. My long cultural history of pomp and circumstance and old-world class had come to an end.

Mary, the young, single home economics teacher, shared my disenchantment. Unruly students and demanding parents drenched our days. We both wanted out. I rented a place directly across the street from the school, spending nights and weekends alone. I would notice Mary dribbling her basketball as she walked past my house, pausing at the walk to my front door. She would stand there slapping the ball back and forth between her hands. Peeking through the sheer curtains on the window, I didn't reach out to her. I really wanted to be with guys.

The following summer, I moved to an apartment in Olathe, a fast-growing suburb on the fringes of the KC metro area. Betsy, another teacher at Wellsville, and Mary carpooled with me each day to school. We each took turns driving. Betsy encouraged us to join a singles Bible study group at a Presbyterian church in Olathe. It opened the door to meeting other singles. Soon a group of us were doing things on weekends and attending Bible study on Wednesday nights. I hesitated before finally confessing to Mom about joining a Protestant church.

Still grieving over my father's death two years previous, she gave her approval when I told her.

"Son, if you've found friends and fellowship, where you go to church doesn't matter. I'm just happy you are going somewhere that keeps you close to God."

The straps of religion and my unreconcilable sexual preference continued to ignite conflict and discontent. As Catholics, we counted on the priest to dictate our beliefs, values, and behavior. The priest deciphered the epistle and gospel during Mass. Now I would explore the Bible in a different environment. The Bible class leader, Barry, tried to mold our religiosity. He would read scripture and then expand on the meaning with his own insights. He constantly referred to Bible readings and his interpretations as the "Word of God." He dated Lisa, a good friend of Betsy's. Betsy was the glue of the Bible study group.

"Most of you are just baby Christians," he assessed. "Since you're probably not able to understand scripture from the Holy Book on your own, all of you need to buy an annotated Bible called 'The Way.'"

This publication's use of everyday words and its reference to "homosexuality" infuriated me and confirmed that this book was not the written word of God. I had researched the word used to describe me and I knew it did not exist at the time of Christ.

This book is a piece of shit and an insult to the real Bible. And who's this guy Barry anyway to call me a baby Christian? I spent more time learning religion by being a good Catholic, an altar boy, and attending a Catholic school than he'll ever know. The ship of my newfound Christianity had just crashed into a giant iceberg of evangelism.

I realized that a couple of the men in the group seemed to be like me as I watched their facial expression while our leader expounded on biblical verses. Jack, a good-looking guy who drove a Corvette, wandered around the room before and after Bible class chatting with the good-looking girls. We became friends and often went to the Sirloin Stockade restaurant on Tuesday for the steak special and then out for a beer.

Barry and Lisa were soon engaged. They announced a Labor Day picnic at Lisa's parents' farmhouse at Wednesday night Bible study. I offered to bring some beer, which was a huge mistake. Silence fell among the group, creating glaring eyes of disappointment.

"Jim, we don't believe in drinking and neither should you. It's a bad thing to choose to do, and it's against God's word. You must strive to be a good Christian," Barry scolded.

What the fuck? Are you shitting me? What in the hell is wrong with drinking? It's bad enough this dumbass state of Kansas only allows 3.2 beer in bars, and now this idiot Barry is trying to tell me it's wrong?

"Well, Barry, I don't think liquor is wrong unless you are

an alcoholic," I asserted. "Are you saying that drinking is a sin according to the Bible? I'm no biblical scholar, but there's an event in the Bible describing Jesus turning water into wine at a wedding ceremony when the host ran out of wine. In fact, the guests asked why the best wine had been saved for last instead of being served at the beginning of the party, the usual custom. And another thing, I can't understand why this church drinks grape juice instead of wine with communion. We drink real wine in the Catholic Church, and I don't think Catholics go against the Bible."

"Let me straighten you out, Jim," Barry snarled. "The reference to wine in the Bible is not alcoholic wine. It's fermented grape juice. God wants us to avoid anything that can be harmful and lead to addiction and bad behavior."

Holy Jesus, I can't believe this bullshit! What in the fuck is fermented grape juice? If it's fermented, it's wine!

"So Barry, you actually think that Kansas should bring back the law now proposed that all liquor must be removed from anyone riding in a train or flying on a plane across Kansas and that no booze should be sold anywhere?" I looked over to Jack thinking he would come to my defense. He just stared down at the open pages of his Bible. Barry surveyed the uneasiness permeating the room before asking the group to pray for the light of God to take me on a path closer to Jesus.

Not wanting to give up the friendships, I did attend the picnic and decided to respect their beliefs even though I thought their logic was insane. Sarah, another member of the group, asked me over for dinner. We had been out several times. She tried to relate to my weakness concerning drinking by admitting everyone had their sins. She also confessed that she worried she had led me on about her feelings toward me. She concluded that we couldn't go out anymore if I were romantically interested in her since she'd been sleeping with another guy in the Bible study and hated herself for it.

The 1980s became a time of change for gays in America, though not for a teacher in Kansas. Harvey Milk, a publicly elected official in San Francisco, and the NYC Stonewall Bar standoff began the movement of gays from all walks of life coming out of the closet. They confronted the NYPD in protest of being hassled for entering and leaving the gay bars.

Anita Bryant, former Miss Oklahoma and second runner-up for Miss America, opposed homosexuality. Using her notoriety as the face of Florida Orange Juice, she became the leader of the religious right and demanded gay teachers be publicly identified and fired. During a confrontation, a pie was thrown in her face. At service the following Sunday, Pastor Bob asked all the congregation to pray for her. I tried to hold my cool but could not help mumbling, "I'm not going to pray for her or her Nazi agenda."

At that moment, a sense of aloneness came over me. My Bible study group all sat in the same pew during Sunday services. To my surprise, looking to my right and then to my left, a huge gap opened between me and the other singles of our group. They had scooted away from me. After church, no one included me in the usual Sunday dinner outing plans. Betsy ignored me at school for weeks. I actually feared for my job if news of this incident got back to Wellsville.

When teaching about the cultural geography of the mid-Atlantic States, I discussed the Amish and their lifestyle. I had talked about how the power and effectiveness of the tradition of shunning had always amazed me. I now knew how it felt firsthand.

One Saturday evening a few weeks later, Jack appeared at my door.

"Jim, a lot of the stuff that goes on in Bible study and church is crazy. I should've stood up for you. You at least had the courage to say what you were thinking. You know what? I think Anita Bryant is a bitch, too. Let's go out for a few beers, I'll be your friend."

"That sounds good to me, Jack."

A few drinks turned into several. When we got back to my place, Jack decided to stay for a few more beers. Instead of sitting across from me in a chair, he sat next to me on the couch. His good looks and bachelor demeanor aroused me as he babbled about his girlfriends.

"You know buddy, I'm fucking a girl in our Bible study. Others fool around too and then they act like they're all high and mighty. I'm on your side about a lot of things...I'm too drunk to drive. Want to crash together? Let's have some fun."

I could tell it was not the first time for Jack to have male sex. He had no trouble being the giver or the receiver.

After Jack left, I took the annotated Bible, "The Way," ripped off the front and back covers, and threw it in the trash. I now knew that skewed interpretations of the Bible by religion and Christian hypocrisy was not for me. I began down the path toward a personal and spiritual relationship with God.

● ● ●

Jack and I would never have sex again even though he was intelligent, traveled, fun, and handsome—everything I wanted in a man. I never suggested another hookup, knowing he dated several girls. Our encounter had been just a fling for him. Complicating our friendship or exposing my preference for guys would destroy my current social world.

Although Betsy and some members of the singles group continued shunning me for several weeks, Mary remained friendly and confided that she didn't agree with their behavior. Though an avid churchgoer, Mary showed compassion and viewed God as less judgmental.

After several weeks of me kissing everyone's ass at Bible study, the cold treatment finally ended with Betsy and her closest friend, Phil, inviting me to spend a few days at the Lake of the Ozarks. Phil's parents offered us the use of the family cabin.

"It'll be fun, Jim, and a chance for you to find your way with God," Betsy concluded. "Phil and I will help you discover that scripture can answer any questions about life."

The Lake of the Ozarks was not far from Moberly, my hometown. It would be nice to get back to Missouri and Lord knew, I needed a vacation that didn't cost much. Discounting the ominous prelude to a religious retreat, I decided the trip would also put me back in the good graces of everyone in the group. Knowing that Mary had been invited helped put me at ease.

The cabin was nestled at the end of a long arm of the huge lake, a reservoir created by the famous Bagnell Dam to provide electricity for most of Missouri. Just beyond the porch of our hideaway extended a long wooden dock, serving several cabins.

"I'm heading down to the lake," I shouted.

"Don't you think we should pray first?" Betsy questioned. "After we get done praying Jim, take the Holy Book with you to the dock and try to learn some verses. I brought one of my Bibles for you to use. If you give the Lord a chance, he'll change your life. Phil and I have our own mission for God to get started on while Mary unpacks and fixes supper. An elder from our Sunday night prayer group has wisely suggested we divide up the Bible by chapters. Each of us should memorize a section in case all Bibles are destroyed if another dictator like Hitler comes along someday. We have to be sure that the word of God is never lost."

Holy Shit! Am I crazy or what? That will never happen in this country, and how in the world can someone memorize a whole chapter in the Bible? I dutifully headed out the door toward the dock. *This vacation is turning into a nightmare. I think I've fucking died and gone to Christian hell.*

I laid down on the edge of the pier, supporting my head with bent elbow as I opened the Bible. The humid summer squelched any desire for learning anything. My attention turned to the big motorboats speeding out to the open water of the lake. People were shouting and laughing. I wanted to be with them instead of "mature Christians."

When Mary finally called that supper was ready, my lazy day snoozing in the sun abruptly ended. Time to face the firing squad.

Walking into the cabin, I let the screen door slam, interrupting Phil's recitation of his assigned scripture chapter. *Jiminy Christmas, he really did it! The fucker must have a photographic memory.*

When he finished, Betsy turned to me, "We did our work for

the Lord today. How did you do?"

"Ugh—well, you're not going to believe this, but, as I looked for verses to learn, I just started thinking about God and life. It's like God and I had a nice, long chat." *Jesus, I hope they fall for this bullshit.*

"Thank you, Jesus," Phil shouted.

"Praise the Lord," Betsy exclaimed as they both held their arms extended in the air with palms facing up. "Let's pray and thank Jesus for this wonderful day."

"Come join us, Mary," Phil commanded.

Mary's eye caught mine as she knelt on the floor and crossed her legs under her, following Betsy's and Phil's lead.

This was not going to be the vacation of a lifetime.

CHAPTER 22

DON'T TELL ME; SHOW ME

Living in Olathe and commuting to Wellsville every morning made for long days. I hated getting up early for the carpool, and I dreamed of sleeping late when I retired, but I still wake up at the same time. Discovering that not all rural communities have well-behaved students and having to teach junior high students made me dread each day.

When lecturing or leading discussions, I often stood in front of the first seat of the center aisle of students. One day, I was explaining an event in seventh grade American history. To my astonishment, the minister's daughter, who sat in the front seat, reached up and outlined my personal area with her fingers without touching. I detested all the immature behavior of that age group. Because the school was small. I taught the primary social studies class for grades 7-12. The senior high students were no better and the opposite of my wonderful students at Highland High, which was my first and my most favorite teaching experience.

Olathe, located just across the southwest border of Kansas City, was the city's fastest-growing suburb. It boasted a large high school with plans for another. A counselor at Olathe High lived in the same apartment complex as I did, and we became friends. When she mentioned there was an opening for a psychology instructor, I thought that it would be a chance to start over and earn better pay.

Luckily, the department chairperson attended the same church as me, and her husband was a Bible study leader and mentored my dreaded singles Bible group. Now was my chance to capitalize on my hours of church attendance. Barry, the young leader of my class, mentioned to the husband of the department chairperson that I had applied for the high school job. He introduced me to her the following Sunday after church.

"It's hard to find a good psychology major that is willing to teach the advanced psychology course we are planning to offer next year," Rosa emphasized. She was a woman of immense status. She had been in the military and succeeded in a man's world. More importantly, she had more power than the principal. After I knew she had talked to the principal, I called his office. Just giving my name to the principal's secretary got me right in for the interview.

By this time, I had started to see a guy, Kip, in Kansas City on weekends, only an hour drive from Wellsville. For once, companionship and caring accompanied sex. Usually, my ventures to gay bars in the city were just for sex. He had a "girlfriend" named Tonya, an awesome gal. The three of us often went out together. I knew that the principal at Olathe, during my interview, would ask the dreaded question: Do you have a girlfriend? I complained to Kip and Tonya that this question could be the end of my chances to teach in Olathe.

"Why don't I go with you to the interview?" Tonya said. "I have a solitaire diamond ring that I can wear, and we can pretend to be engaged."

She played the part perfectly. When the principal smiled at me when introducing my fiancée, I knew the job was mine. I taught in Olathe until my retirement in 2005, though living out my homosexuality on society's terms. I didn't come out of the closet until moving to California.

Everything happened as planned, and with the Department Chair's insistence, the job rolled into my lap. Olathe was the world headquarters of the Nazarene Church, and there seemed to be a church on every street corner. But I believed being close to Kansas City would mean that people would have more cosmopolitan attitudes and students would be more interested in academics. I wanted to believe that my new surroundings would also allow me to be understood and accepted.

• • •

It was almost ten in the morning, near the end of third-period geography class. My tummy yearned for those powdered sugar donut gems sitting next to my name plaque. They would be devoured over morning break. This had been a good week—no hall duty or student smoking area assignment during the break. It would be a fun 15 minutes with friends in the teacher's lounge.

I had adjusted as much as possible to not being married and not having children. I would never be able to talk about children I did not have; what they were doing; how beautiful they were growing up. I would never have a wife dropping in at school with the kids. Enjoyable interaction with favorite friends at school helped fill the gap of lonely times.

I especially enjoyed my friendship with Lisa, the Xerox lady. We sometimes would get to laughing so hard, the principal would look into the copy room to see what was going on. It's ironic how we automatically think people we are close to will be on the same page on personal beliefs. Lisa was so "hip" that I almost felt no need to disguise my guy problems with "she's" in our dialogue about my dating experiences.

It was a scary time to be gay. People had just begun to drop like flies from AIDS. So little was known about the disease. Some even thought you could get it by drinking from the same container. One thing for sure, HIV was a death sentence. I needed the intimacy with men, yet I was scared of dying alone and the disgrace it would bring to my family. Sex was an intense approach/ avoidance life conflict. I needed the support and empathy of a straight friend and Lisa was my mentor in life.

"Wow, Lisa, this AIDS thing is scary, don't you think?" I eased back on the sofa behind her face to avoid eye contact.

She lit her long Virginia Slims cigarette as it dangled on one side of her mouth. She began to speak in a convinced derogatory tone, "Oh, Jim, that plague is just God's way of dealing with homosexuals. The Lord must punish queers for their sinful behavior. They are outright perverted and breaking the word of the Bible." I began to drown in shock, observing other teachers saying nothing and okay with her stance.

"Come on my friend, do you think God punishes people that don't even choose who they are?" Within a few minutes, I was able to come up with a reason for her flawed opinion, "What about babies born to infected mothers who die as babies, never getting to live?"

Lisa didn't hesitate in her response. "Jim, it's not a Christian's business to question the way God deals with disgusting behavior and sin. If babies are hit, it's just what has to happen to fulfill God's plan."

Lisa's assessment will always be lodged in my brain and the deep emotional pain of desertion by a friend showed me that sometimes you really don't know a person. She was not alone, President Reagan, considered at the time a great president, dismissed pleas by the surgeon general to find a cure, proclaiming the disease would only kill the homosexuals.

● ● ●

The sky was cold and completely gray, typical of Kansas in February 1984. Flecks of snow hit Mary Hilda on her cheeks as she stepped out of the secondary doors heading outside from the church vestibule. The severe chill in the air seemed to freeze the teardrops on her cheeks. She looked straight down in order not to miss or slip on the first icy step leading down the long flight of stairs to the sidewalk below. Mary graciously accepted the comfort of her husband holding her arm as he also fought back the pain and tears to be strong for his wife.

The casket and pallbearers moved carefully but quickly down

the steep incline of each step. Andy, a once golden-brown headed sweet young man of twenty-three years would soon be lifted into the black limousine. Flowers adorned every window. Andrew, an honors graduate of the University of Kansas, had possessed a classy, extroverted style and a love to help others; therefore, he had chosen nursing as his career.

Mary paused at the bottom of the steps to watch her son be lifted in the back of the limo. Thoughts of her son, soon to be laid to rest forever, tormented her as the procession prepared to leave. Her husband encouraged her not to succumb to the protesters that were present across the street. It was impossible not to hear the famous anti-homosexual church activists as they shouted and milled about. They stood the exact number of feet away as prescribed by Topeka city ordinance. The signs pierced Mary Hilda's heart as she read each one, "Your son is going straight to Hell," "God sends faggots to burn for eternity," "God hates queers," and "AIDS is for homosexuals." As the line of vehicles proceeded beyond the shouts, Mary had to endure each cry of hate as Andy was lowered in his grave.

Time nor knowledge has changed some of the perceptions of behavior regarding homosexuals. Relatively recently on The Oprah Winfrey Show, Joel Osteen commented that homosexuals were not God's best work. She had reached out to him as a friend to address concerns as to financial questions concerning his church. As he made the statement, Oprah sat in silence and offered no comment.

If Jesus Christ were alive today, would he question his Father's work?

• • •

As HIV spiraled, I feared contracting the disease. My father was gone, and my mother would be left with the stigma. Small town gossip would destroy my mother. "Did you know Irene's son died from AIDS? I always knew he was queer." My brother would be angry, and my grandmother would not even understand. My family would be strapped with the judgment of old-world values and Catholic church dogma.

Though I feared dying from a painful and prolonged disease, I could not let my mother be hurt and needed an alternative to dying without stigma. I decided the Catholic denouncement of suicide was secondary. I had already begun to doubt Hell as described by the church. In case I died of AIDS, I had a plan to hide the real reason for my death.

After long deliberations, I thought of a way to make my death nonviolent and not appear to be suicide. I would do it before the disease progressed so nobody would know I'd had AIDS.

Get drunk as hell on vodka
Leave partially chopped vegetables in the kitchen sink
Hold a potato loosely in the palm of my hand
Pour vodka all over my wrist
Let the butcher knife slip onto my arteries
Faint and die
Everyone will think you were too drunk to be cutting up vegetables
This will work
Jim, can you do this?
Yes, I can and I will

With the no tolerance regarding getting the homosexual plague, many of my friends had their own ways to escape the humiliation of dying from AIDS.

• • •

Being a homosexual teacher in a very religiously intolerant community was lonely. There was no one to share gay thoughts and experiences on a daily basis. Appearing in public too often with guys or recognizing a fellow teacher as gay could mean the end of a career. My "gaydar" signaled that Gerald was a "sister." He would often come by my room to chat and drop hints. After many "what-ifs" he suggested a drink at my place sometime.

I had come to know his wife from faculty get-togethers. Not

only was adultery bad karma, but also against the law in many states even if you were not the one married. I nicely declined the offer knowing his motivations. On another occasion, he asked if he could entertain a friend at my home rather being seen at a motel with a guy. I had to say no because I treasured my house as my "home" and private to me. I could tell he felt let down.

Whenever there came an impromptu announcement for a faculty meeting after school, it usually meant bad news. At this emergency meeting, the principal announced that Gerald had resigned and left the building. The rumor was that he had been arrested by a policeman for "public display of affection" at a rest stop. Originally, the officer was not going to charge him until he saw Gerald marching with his Scout group at The Old Settlers Day Parade. Patrolmen often monitored rest areas to catch homosexuals. He did not even arrest Gerald until after the fact as the parade was several days later. The quick-spreading gossip included information that the participant with Gerald was the son of a policeman. The officer supposedly said he would not have arrested them if he hadn't thought that Gerald would molest boys in his Scout troop. I felt some guilt in that I had let Gerald down.

• • •

I loved my students and always tried to protect and help them succeed academically. I could always identify if a student was gay or struggling with it.

Olathe North, the school where I'd taught for over 20 years, had always had one of the best football teams in Kansas. Winning the state championship was a common occurrence. Football was almighty. The debate coach, a proclaimed born-again Christian, did a verbal skit during the Friday morning announcements over the intercom predicting "Eagle" victory. He proclaimed to be the "phantom eagle." One Friday, we were playing a school with the mascot, The Stags. The debate instructor announced, "The Eagles will beat Bishop Miege as they are a bunch of fa.."

I became outraged knowing gay students sitting in any

classroom were being ridiculed for who they were. Storming into the debate coach's room, I demanded an apology on the announcements the following Monday or I would turn his skit off in the future. Within minutes, an assistant principal came to my room to sit with my students and demanded me to report to the principal's office immediately.

Entering the office, the head principal slammed the door behind me and ordered me to sit down. He was a macho jock type, proud of his high school football days. I actually thought he was going to hit me as he leaned across his desk to be in my face. Surprising myself, I said, "Your scare tactics don't work with me. You may be able to scare the female teachers, but not me. You take the first punch, and I guarantee I will take the next one."

For several weeks to follow, a vice-principal would come to my room to make sure I didn't censor the "phantom eagle." No kind of apology was ever made to the student body. There was no formal write-up on my behavior. I knew my job was only saved due to Kansas law that made it difficult to fire a tenured teacher. For one of the first times in my adult life, I felt self-worth and pride.

Later in my career, I had another encounter which required personal pride and determination to fight discrimination and oppression. I heard the Superintendent of Olathe Public Schools had walked into the library at Olathe North High School and asked the librarian to bring him the book entitled Annie on My Mind from the stacks. He walked away from the control desk and out of the room with the book.

The book centered on the life of a lesbian student finding her way in life. Only a few students had checked the book out. The following day after the news of the book being pulled, I called the superintendent in protest of its removal. In my rant, I reminded the Superintendent that there is a process to place a book on the shelf and a process to remove it. It was properly put in circulation after its contribution by a gay rights organization. I reminded him that he violated the guidelines to remove a book. I also expressed my opinion that he acted out of pressure from the religious right in Olathe.

Fortunately, one of a few broad-minded parents allowed their daughter to file a lawsuit under the guidance of the ACLU. The school district spent a huge sum of potential educational funds to fight the case. They lost, and I heard the book was removed again after the courts reinstated the book. Supposedly, the school board amended the book removal policy and proceeded to ban the book from the library as it was supplied by a special rights group. The policy didn't seem to apply to the steady stream of Bibles supplied to the district.

• • •

My life as a homosexual was a minefield of hatred, violence, and degradation. One of the scariest nights in my life took place on a Saturday night in the late 1980s. As I approached a gay bar on Broadway Street in downtown KC, I found a parking spot directly across the street from a gay nightclub.

After locking my car and checking for traffic, I proceeded to cross the four-lane street. About a third of the way across the street, a speeding car approached me and slammed on its breaks and stopped directly in front of me. One of the guys in the car shouted, "Get in if you want to go with us and suck our big dicks." Though that normally sounded interesting, I felt this was not a good situation and these guys were not just looking for fun. A force outside of my body was dictating my behavior. A guy started to get out of the car as if to throw me into their car.

I knew death awaited me. With a sudden surge of energy and avoidance reaction, I hurled myself over the hood of the car. My body traveled more than the normal distance of a hurling jump. I landed completely across the street not giving the car the ability to run me over. Pulling myself up to run, I noticed I didn't have a scrape or scratch. As they drove by one of them shouted, "You better pray on those knees instead of giving blowjobs. God hates queers." A gunshot rang out as I entered the bar.

It had taken a higher power to show me that I was wanted and meant to be alive in this world.

145

CHAPTER 23

THE BICYCLE AND THE NEW ROAD TAKEN

As the old saying goes, enough is enough. I had my fill of boredom, no fun, and the righteous social life of two-faced people. My return to the real world still did not include living a gay lifestyle. As a teacher, being gay could lead to being fired. I found myself caught in the limbo of needing male companionship and sex, yet wanting a family.

Overland Park, an expanding suburb of KC had taken the initiative and passed a "liquor by the drink" ordinance in the 1980s, which gave rise to many nightclubs. Much of Kansas allowed only private clubs to serve hard liquor from a bottle purchased by a club member and stored on a designated spot on the shelf. My favorite nightclub, The Penthouse, on the top floor of a Ramada Inn, was a swinging nightspot in Johnson County, Kansas.

I now could experience the things I enjoyed in straight life and pursue the opportunity to meet guys. Dancing "The Bump" with good-looking girls and chatting and mingling with an in-crowd brought me joy and a feeling of normalcy. I proudly owned at least 10 leisure suits with matching acetate shirts and pointed collars that draped down on the outside of the suit jackets. I purchased every color of the cheap suits at Woolco, and I took pride in being known as a great "bumper."

I tried to live out the other side of me in 'straight' surroundings. When not dancing, I would sit at the bar with other men, looking for the opportunity to meet someone. Many men in those days who were gay or swung both ways would never go to a gay bar. Sitting next to an attractive guy could lead to "accidental" touching of one leg to another, followed by intentional rubbing of each other's leg. Getting lucky and asked up to a guy's hotel room or an apartment satisfied a real craving in my life. To this day, I remember one man who always sat next to me and aroused intense emotion and physical desire in me. Many times, he would suggest breakfast after the nightclub closed, yet never made a move to indicate an interest in intimacy. It's so true in life that now and then a person comes along that instantly steals every aspect of your being. You never forget him, even if it's just a brief encounter.

One evening, I noticed a table of unfamiliar girls. One girl with long, straight, blonde hair caught my eye. Blonde hair always made practicing heterosexuality easier for me. Her quick acceptance to dance and her attractiveness threw me back into my heterosexual mode. I found out her name was Liz. She had a high-level position with Hallmark Cards, one of Kansas City's most prestigious home-based corporations. I always thought getting a job with Hallmark would be wonderful. We would do dinner and a movie every Saturday and sometimes out to eat on Friday, too, which quickly drained my teacher's budget. I knew she was not an ordinary girl, and thoughts of marriage and family soon displaced shallow encounters with guys.

I knew things were getting serious when she asked me to her home in Omaha, Nebraska, to meet her mother. My feelings for Liz were genuine, and a dream family life would mean more to me than anything, even if it meant giving up guys.

Liz offered to cook dinner to celebrate my birthday. I thought it strange she didn't want to take me to my favorite restaurant.

Maybe she just wants to show me that she is a good cook as well as being a corporate tycoon. And maybe dessert will be a trip up to the bedroom to finally go all the way.

Walking into the living room, I noticed a spanking new beautiful, black English Racer bicycle next to the fireplace. *Wow, look at that bike! She has really gone all out for me. That must have cost 300 bucks. Would have been nice if she had just put a big bow on the handlebars.*

"Liz, that's a beautiful bicycle." I walked over to run my hands over the leather seat. "Isn't it great, Jim? I went out shopping today to get you a birthday present, and when I saw the bike, I couldn't resist getting it. I've always wanted a racer. I didn't find a birthday present for you, though. We can get you something the next time we're out and about."

Well, bite me in the ass. Are you shitting me? After all the money I have spent on her, all this time together, going to meet her mom, and not getting any sex, she comes up with a bike for herself and nothing for my birthday? Not even a fucking bottle of cologne!

"I've got to check on supper, Jim."

I held my hand to my forehead. "Liz, I've picked up one of my sinus headaches all of a sudden. I'm going to pass on dinner and head home." I quickly bolted out the door not giving her a chance to respond.

Slamming my hand on the car roof before opening the front door of my car, I looked up to the sky and shouted, "I am fucking through with women. Men, look out! Here I come!"

I plopped down in the front seat of my car feeling a wonderful sense of freedom to finally explore the real me. I decided to find a better place than straight nightclubs to meet guys. Having been to adult bookstores to buy gay porn, I had noticed a book called *The Worldwide Damron Travel Guide for Gay Sex.* After gathering the information needed, my goal was to give myself a fantastic 27th birthday present.

Standing in front of the gay magazine section, I looked over to see that the guide cost $9.95. Deciding it cost too much, I explored the book by pretending to be browsing its contents before purchasing. I quickly began to flip pages to find the section on Kansas City.

Suddenly, a guy standing next to me tapped the side of my foot with his. When I looked over at him, he made eye contact with me. Although an older guy, probably around 40, he caught my attention with his nice, clean-cut looks. I eagerly smiled back at him. He immediately motioned to the back of the store with his head before walking to the front counter to hand some money to the clerk. He proceeded to the back hallway. I followed him down the dimly lit hall passing closed doors with lights above each entrance indicating they were occupied. It reminded me of confessionals at church that identified confessions in progress in the same manner.

My pursuer quickly dashed into an empty room leaving the door open for me to enter. He pushed the door shut, trapping me. A single, exposed lightbulb dimly lit the room. The stench of stale sex and lingering cigarette smoke permeated the air. I kicked a used condom to the corner, feeling my shoes stick to the floor from dried semen. Confinement to this sex dungeon smothered any hope in my soul that I would be proud of my behavior tomorrow.

The masculine guy with salt and pepper hair and a Cary Grant appearance began to touch me below my belt stirring me to sexual arousal despite my frightening feelings of inexperience.

"Hi, how are you? My name is Marty." I reached to shake his hand, then quickly pulled back realizing it was a stupid gesture.

"Whatever," the guy mumbled as he began to unzip my pants.

"Are you here to meet guys?" I asked

"Look, buddy, that's obvious, isn't it? I'm not here to get to know you or answer a hundred questions. I'm a married guy just looking to suck dick."

The news that he was married doused any excitement he had stirred in my pants.

"So, what's wrong?" he grumbled, his demeanor beginning to show frustration.

"Well, aren't we committing adultery?"

"Look, man, I'm the one committing adultery if you want to call it that. Good grief, I am just sucking you off, not screwing you. I've paid for the room. You want to do this or not?"

Feeling guilty about his expenditure and looking at his handsome face, I found myself caught up in the situation and let things unfold. After we finished, I rushed out of the store to my car. All the way home, my Catholic morality told me I had just sinned.

This is a real sin. You broke one of the Ten Commandments, not just a no-no from a Bible study leader manipulating words from the Bible. The Bible is not the word of God, but the Commandments are. Something in me always made me feel that God appeared to Moses through a burning bush to give the world guidelines to live by. Besides that, I knew when my behavior felt wrong in my heart and mind, it was wrong. That guy back there says he's the one committing adultery, what about the other Commandment that "thou shall not covet another man's wife"? I just coveted a wife's man.

Journeying down the new road of being 100 percent homosexual, I became jaded and twisted. My new morality rationalized what I wanted to do. I ventured the wrong way down a one-way street with married guys. Each time I broke my moral code, guilt and bad karma followed. I learned the truths in life about married guys who have affairs:

They will keep their secret until you are hooked.

You are always there for them; they are never there for you.

You will find yourself alone on holidays, birthdays, and Saturday nights.

They will tell you every lie in the world to convince you that everything is okay and that you are doing the right thing.

"If it's not you, it'll be someone else, but I want to be with you."

"Try and understand, I didn't know I was gay when I got married. I need to be with a guy."

"My wife doesn't like sex anymore, so it's right that we have that with each other."

"I'm going to leave my wife someday, I'm only happy when I'm with you."

Bullshit. Complete bullshit.

On my next trip to the bookstore, I found a list of gay bars as well as two other places in the sex guide to meet guys in Kansas City. Gay bars did not seem like an option since I might run into someone from my school. Two places caught my eye as rendezvous spots: cruising the Country Club Plaza by car after 1 a.m. and the Liberty Memorial Mall. I found it hard to believe these two famous and cherished places in Kansas City also played host to men meeting men.

I decided on the Liberty Memorial as the first place to try and meet a guy. I loved its crisp art deco structure with its phallic symbolic appearance. A tree-lined boulevard led up to the largest monument and museum in America honoring WWI veterans. A ride on the enclosed elevator to the top of the multi-sided pillar gave a panoramic view of downtown KC. The eternal flame symbolized the bravery and valor of fallen soldiers. The flowering trees and bushes covering the mall were especially beautiful in early spring.

One Saturday night, I finally had the courage to parallel park along the mall boulevard. Keeping my window down would be an invitation for guys to stop and talk. Finally, a guy paused to check me out. After a brief chat, he suggested a walk down the hill.

His thick, coarse, blondish hair and crinkled eyes enhanced his boyish appeal. He spoke softly but with an assuredness that oozed from his broad shoulders and Southern accent.

Thinking he was a nice guy; I began to hope that we would have sex and then date; the standard routine with gay men.

Finding a secluded spot, he drew me in close to kiss me. The scent of his Polo cologne made the cool night air even more crisp and exhilarating. His lips gently touched mine before he began to deeply open-mouth kiss. He kissed me like I had been taught by my wild girlfriend in high school. He ignited fire and passion in my heart more powerful than any other aspect of sex. I will always remember this as my first real kiss with a man. One thing led to another and soon our pants were open. Suddenly, he pulled away and began to secure his jeans.

"Look out," he warned. "Someone's coming up the hill, it could be a cop."

I quickly began to zip-up my pants. "Ouch. Oh my God, my dick is stuck in my zipper."

"Goddamn," my trick shouted. "Why do you think gay guys wear button down Levi's 501s? Pull your shirt down. Let's get out of here." He buttoned up his jeans and bolted away. I hobbled to my car.

No matter what I did, it hurt like hell. Sitting down in my car finally relieved the pressure. I decided to take a deep breath and give a quick yank to free myself. The effort proved hopeless and the pain unbearable. I knew my only choice was the emergency room at St. Mary's hospital on Main Street just across from the Memorial.

When I reached the emergency room check-in, I tried to fill out the paperwork while concealing my problem with my jacket.

"Sir, you need to go sit down in a chair and fill out this paperwork instead of standing here."

"Ummm," I whispered to the nurse as I leaned over the counter, "Ma'am, please help me. My penis is caught in my pants zipper. I can't sit down."

"Sir, have you been drinking?" she asked. "Well, anyway, I'll let you come on into the treatment area to finish the paperwork."

I felt so embarrassed as I laid on the bed in the emergency room. I strategically placed my hand over myself to conceal my predicament.

"Mr. Ros—teel—o, you're going to have to remove your hand from your penis so I can check the bleeding," the ER nurse demanded.

"Can't I just wait for the doctor?" I pleaded.

"Look, sir, you aren't the first guy in here with his penis stuck in his zipper, lift your hand."

Reluctantly, I slipped my hand away feeling like the whole world knew every intimate detail about me. I finally left the hospital with two stitches and wearing loose-fitting surgical scrubs that the kind doctor gave me.

About a month later, I decided to try cruising streets on the Country Club Plaza in Kansas City after 1:00 a.m. as suggested in the sex guide. Constructed in the 1920s as the first suburban open-air shopping center in the United States, it soon became the pride of Kansas City. Built as a sister city to Seville, Spain, each building on the Plaza oozed with Spanish charm and architecture. Most visitors tout this venue as unsurpassed by any other shopping district in the country. Each building is outlined with lights at Christmas and is ranked as the best holiday light show in the United States.

The cat and mouse game of following someone around the Plaza several times sometimes resulted in detours to dark and quiet streets. Chats were superficial and mostly unproductive with only a couple of interludes. One evening, shortly before midnight I spotted a fellow teacher in his Jeep, with its top-down, driving around the Plaza. That scared me from ever cruising there again. I finally decided a gay bar was the only chance to meet guys interested in dating and friendship as well as sex.

After my encounter with the zipper and shallow hook-ups, I decided to visit a gay bar called the Dover Fox that I found in the *Damron Sex Guide*. It took all my courage to finally walk into the bar knowing I could be spotted by someone connected to my teaching job. I convinced myself that anyone exposing me would be admitting they were there also. The hardest thing for me to accept was knowing that my new road meant marriage and family would never happen. A good talk with myself gave me the courage to accept this limitation in my life. *Jim, at least you are with kids every day as a teacher, changing lives and building good memories. Some of your students back at Highland are doing well in life and keeping in touch, thanking you for your influence in their lives.*

The moment I walked into that bar in Kansas City, I knew it would offer me the chance to be true to myself and find the right guys to enjoy life with. I never felt so 'not alone' in a room of strangers. Seeing men hugging, laughing, and dancing to the beat of the music as mist drifted up from the dance floor eased any of my concerns about being there. The scent of cologne and men's deodorant soap drifted in the air. While standing on the sideline of the dancing men, I heard my favorite song: Turn the Beat Around, begin to play. The entire bar emptied onto the pulsating lighted disco dance stage. Within a moment, a cute guy grabbed my arm and led me deep into the crowd. We began to dance in sync, my arms flailing in the air to the beat of the music.

Turn it up, turn it upside down,
Turn the beat around,
Love to hear percussion,
Love to hear it.

Dancing with him stirred in me spiraling exhilaration and fulfillment. For the first time, I felt normal. Going to cocktail hours and finding guys in business suits proved to me that anyone could be gay and still be part of all walks of life. I quickly found myself entwined in the gay culture, including stopping for a pack of cigarettes to smoke at the bar. Holding them in just the right way and exhaling with the right turn of the head gave me a feeling of stability in who I had become and where life was taking me.

On just my fourth or fifth visit to The Dover Fox, I looked around the room to check out guys while sipping my rum and Coke with lime. In a far corner, with a drink in hand and sitting alone on a bar stool, I saw Dan, the resident assistant from my dormitory at college. I couldn't believe my eyes. He stood out in my vision like the North Star on a cold clear night. My heart fell to my gut like a boulder off a cliff. My thoughts raced with déjà vu of all the times we had laughed and talked, our eyes communicating our undisclosed love. Though many years had passed, I loved him at that moment with the same intensity as the first time we had passed each other in the hallway of our dorm.

Did he move to Kansas City from his farm near Des Moines? My God, he has no way of knowing I am here. What should I do? What if he's waiting for his date? What if he doesn't feel like he used to for me?

I downed my drink and hurried to the bar service area to get another one. I needed time to think about what to do next. While watching the bartender squeeze the lime before dropping it in my drink, I felt someone's fingers pressing the back of my neck while his thumb gripped close to my collarbone. I turned quickly to free myself only to stare into Dan's glacier blue eyes. He still had that earthy, handsome farm boy face and a message in his smile that nothing had changed between us.

"So, it's my little Giuseppe from college."

Those were the only words I really needed to hear. Our conversation that night of where we had been and what we had done filled the distance of passed time. Now, we had no barriers to keep us apart. We embraced. I outlined his face with my fingers while he held his hand behind my ear before playing with my hair. I buried my head on his shoulders as he held me close: the things we could never do in college days.

I didn't want to be separated from him even long enough for him to follow me home.

We moved his car to a well-lit spot on the street and he drove my car to my place. We were both so emotionally drained, I promised to show him my house in the morning. We headed to the bedroom. Kissing seemed hard for him, so I didn't pursue the thing I wanted most. His body was all I could ask for. The years of farming gave him strength in his touch. I loved his beautiful, circumcised manhood, my preference in the gay world of likes and dislikes. That night we shared with each other in every way, except the most intimate thing. I had been on the top with several guys during man-to-man penetration. It seemed the guys wanted that under any circumstances while I wanted to give that to someone special in the right situation. Dan stirred the desire in me to give him my virginity. But I soon discovered that neither intercourse nor kissing would ever happen between us. He was only interested in receiving oral sex.

For the next few months, Dan came to my home in Olathe. Being together grew easy for us. He was mostly a white T-shirt and jeans type of guy. I enjoyed just relaxing and having him with me. When I would suggest a movie or a local bite to eat, he became more nervous than me about going anywhere in public close to Olathe. He feared it could affect my job.

Our physical intimacy became stagnant and routine, but my love for him outweighed his uptight feelings about sex.

"I do love you, my buddy." he would often tell me. "I just don't feel right about having sex. I think I feel guilty about it. And it's not masculine."

His visits became further apart. He had a small apartment in Des Moines. He had only come to KC on weekends, but never encouraged me to drive up to see him. Finally, one Thursday, he seemed okay with me coming up for the weekend. I reveled in excitement until I discovered a small leak in my gas tank after noticing a puddle in my driveway. My mechanic warned me that highway driving could be dangerous. He could not fix it until the following Monday. Being young, stupid, and in love, I drove to Des Moines to see Dan anyway. He was angry that I did such a risky thing just to come up for a few days. He ended up holding me tight and promised to help get the gas tank fixed on Monday morning after I called in sick to work.

"What's wrong, Dan?" I asked after he pulled away from our usual oral fun later in the day.

"Jim, you deserve more than what I'm able to give you. I just can't do the things I know you need and want from me. I'm okay with knowing I love you, but sex with a guy just doesn't seem right, especially kissing and stuff. My family would never understand me being with a guy and doing those things. Being together would be hard for your mom, too, and what about your job? High school kids can be brutal about you being gay and they can make your life miserable."

I began to plead, "I love you so much. I could tell my mom anything with you standing next to me. If I had to change jobs or move, I'd do that for you. If we had to live in a tent, I'd be happy as long as we were together."

"You say that now Jim, but don't put me over anyone else when I'm not even happy with who I am."

"Dan, we were destined to be together since the first day we met in college."

"Baby, I know that, but what is meant to be is not always able to be. You need to find someone who can give you what I can't. You deserve that. Then, if you make choices that change your life, you've done it for the right person."

I threw my clothes and things into my duffle bag and headed to my car, holding back the tears until I was a block away. I cried the entire trip home, thinking it would be okay if my car blew up from the gas leak and ended my misery.

It took me all this time to finally admit I'm gay and to find a guy to love. First, I can't make love work with a woman, and now I can't keep the love of a guy. So, I'll never have someone to love and never have a family either. I'll never get over Dan, and I'm done with ever hoping to be with someone in life.

The road traveled to discover who I was and fulfill my need to love and be loved had come to a dead end.

Soon, I was speeding down the highway of one-night stands.

CHAPTER 24

BLESSED VIRGINITY

My emotional reaction to love lost, or maybe never found, manifested itself in promiscuity. During the anger stage of my grief, after the initial shock and heartbreak of losing Dan, good sex with anyone became my way to compensate for the loneliness and despair of not finding a partner.

At 28, I remained a virgin homosexual. I had been 'top' with several guys, but, always hesitant to be the receiver. It wasn't because I didn't want to; it became more about wanting it to be with someone I loved. Wondering how it would feel and if it would hurt also deterred me. Being 'bottom' with a guy would be the last step in facing up to my true sexuality. I had avoided it until being exclusively gay. As a top, I could tell myself I really couldn't be gay if I weren't into getting penetrated. With being out of control after my breakup with Dan, my drive to discover that part of sex teased my thoughts. It would be my way to tell the world that I could survive with just sex.

Can it feel as good as most of the guys I have topped claim it to be? It does seem kinda exciting to feel what a girl does with a guy. Come to think of it, you did get so excited about girls getting it by the guy in the front or back seat while 'parking' on double-dates in high school.

God, I really think I want it bad. No, I don't think I do. I know I do.

With Dan gone from my life, each trip to the bar intensified the need to try bottom. All the good-looking guys added to my desire to do more. One guy, Bill, especially heightened my interest. His thick uncontrollable golden-brown hair matched his deep sexy brown eyes. His eyes reminded me of a puppy begging for a treat. He appeared to be in his early 20s and possessed hustler quality looks. I would see him leaving the bar time after time with other drop-dead handsome guys.

Damn, he'll probably never give me the time of day. I want him to kiss me so fucking bad and to be the one to take me to another world. Everyone says he's hung like a horse too. Mmm, that scares me, but, what the hell, get real Jim, you don't have a prayer to hook up with him.

Just a couple of Saturday nights later, I walked up to the bar to get a drink. There was enough room to squeeze between Bill and another guy to order my rum and Coke without walking over to the crowded service area. As I hailed the bartender, Bill looked me over and smiled. My heart began to race.

"Hey guy, what's goin' on?" he asked. "I've seen you in here a lot. Where's your boyfriend tonight?"

"I don't have a boyfriend anymore. We broke up a couple of months ago."

"Oh well, I would say it's his loss. You're a cute little guy. I love short guys."

Jesus, did I just hear what I thought I heard? What do I do next?

While my mind stewed in disbelief, I felt his fingers move up from the back of my knee to the top of my thigh. I felt desire for him to fuck me. He then slipped his hand onto my crotch as he looked to the guy on the other side of me, carrying on a conversation with him as well as me. Given his companion's looks, I didn't have a chance.

He turned back toward me, reached out his hand and said, "My name is Bill. And yours?" "I know your name is Bill," I blurted out. *Oh, shit, you dumb fuck. That's the worst thing you could have said!* "My name is Jim," I quickly announced, hoping that admitting I knew his name would go unnoticed.

"So, you already know who I am?"

"Uh … yeah." *Dammit, think fast, Rostello.* "Yeah, I just heard the bartender call you Bill a minute ago when I walked up here to order my drink." *Whew, good thinking, Jim.*

"Well, good to meet you, Jim." He leaned over close to my ear and whispered, "I was flattered for a minute there. Thought you might have been asking other guys about me." Then, he gave me a killer wink.

My heart began to dance thinking this guy might be interested in me.

"So, what are you up to tonight?" Bill asked. "Cruising for some fun? The lights are about to come on for last call, you know."

"Guess, I'll be heading home," I confessed.

"Well, tell me what's on your mind for tonight?" Bill asked, his voice low and provocative. "What kind of action are you looking for? You like to suck and get fucked?"

"The sucking sounds good, I've never been fucked," I mumbled as I looked down at my drink.

"Oh hell," Bill snapped, sitting straight up on his bar stool. "That's a fucking turn on for me. I'll be your first and I'll take you to where you've never been. Let's get the hell out of here."

We both downed our drinks and headed to the door, his hand firmly gripping the back of my neck, guiding me through the dispersing crowd. I felt like the entire bar watched me leave with this gorgeous guy and that was great. No, not just great. It was amazing.

We slipped on our winter coats as we exited the bar. Bill began to walk toward his car.

"We're going to my place," Bill demanded. "Follow me till you see me park, then park behind me."

Neither one of us said anything as I followed him up the stairs and passed the common area of the apartment complex. The covered pool and scattered patches of snow reminded me that summer would be months away. We both had had way too much to drink. As Bill fumbled to unlock the door to his place, I noticed the number nine on his apartment #19 didn't have a nail on the bottom and hung crooked. I began to jiggle it as Bill struggled to get the deadbolt and door lock simultaneously unlocked. When the door finally opened, I realized the blaring television I heard came from his apartment.

"Your TV is on. You don't live alone?"

"It's cool, buddy. I just don't like coming home to a quiet house," Bill explained.

His apartment looked like a disaster zone from a tornado. Shoes everywhere, a multitude of dirty drinking glasses occupied the coffee table. Magazines and newspapers covered the kitchen counter. The sink in the small utility kitchen overflowed with dirty dishes and several days of coffee mugs vied for space on the table.

"Make yourself at home, little buddy," Bill offered.

"There's no room on the sofa," I said, looking at the heap of clothes covering the entire surface of the couch.

"Yeah, I just did laundry earlier tonight." Bill scooped up the clothes and tossed them on the floor behind the sofa. "You drink rum and Coke, right?" Bill asked as he headed for the kitchen.

"I'll have whatever you've got. Dang, it's freezing in here." I said, hesitating to take off my coat.

"Ah, shit, the gas company has cut me off again, so the furnace isn't working." He walked over to the electric range in the kitchen, turned on all the top burners. He threw open the oven door, exposing an already glowing heating element. "That should help in a few minutes. Good thing the electricity is included in the rent. Let's just go to the bedroom and get warm."

The bedroom seemed in no better shape. The bed looked like it had not been made-up for days. Pillows with head impressions were scattered all over it, and there was even one on the floor.

"Get comfortable," Bill said as he placed our drinks on the night table next to the bed. I took a long gulp of my drink before taking off my clothes but leaving my underwear on. We jumped in bed quickly to get under the covers. I quickly learned that what I had heard about Bill was true as he undressed. He slowly eased in bed, moving close to hold me. The minute he looked into my eyes and began to kiss me, all of my doubts melted into intense physical desire. I suddenly felt like I was floating on satin sheets. Like a suite at the Ritz, the atmosphere was warm and inviting.

Bill wasted no time in removing my briefs and tossing them on the floor. His looks, his body, and his aggressiveness took me to a place I had never been. As he began to work his way down my body with his mouth, I felt his hand moving strategically behind me. Within a moment, he reached where I wanted him to be with his fingers.

"That feels so damn good," I whispered in his ear.

"Yeah, it's that old whore's trick to get her john off, but you just hold tight buddy, I'm going to take you to heaven. I'm going to do what a woman can't do with just her fingers. When I'm done, you'll never forget me."

Passion and raw physical attraction took away any thoughts of how this might hurt. He started slow, and when I began to wince, he just kept going, kissing me harder and deeper. I reached the screaming moment of release quickly without touching myself, and I felt his body move in sync with mine in those uncontrollable seconds. He waited for nature to take its course before moving away.

"That was so fucking good, Jim." He pulled me close and I rested my head on his chest.

All I could think about was how good I felt, though still in pain. *How can hurt feel so good?* It wasn't long until I heard someone coming into the apartment. "Bill ... Bill, wake up. Someone's breaking in."

"It's just my roommate. He'll sleep on the couch for a while, or he might fuck you, too."

Realizing that this was an unkempt one-bedroom apartment made me feel like a cheap slut.

"No, I think I'd better go," I said, easing out of bed to search for my underwear.

"Well, hope you had a good time, buddy."

I walked out to find this gorgeous guy fixing himself a drink. After looking me over, he asked me if I wanted a drink. By this time, Bill had come into the room. We all looked at each other several times. I went from a virgin to a slut in one night.

After it was all over, I became overwhelmed with disappointment. I couldn't muster a word while putting on my clothes. I didn't want to hear the answers to my unasked questions.

As I was getting into my car, the cold winter night air did not bother me as much as usual. I waited for the car defroster to clear the windshield. The cold car seat actually felt good against my soreness. It reminded me of the wonderful moments of uncharted love. I would never forget Bill, though he had probably already forgotten me.

My innocence had been thrown to an intrusive suitor. His good looks and porn star endowment was supposed to make me feel lucky, but all I felt was disappointment.

The next time we saw each other at the bar, he gave me only a passing glance. That's the way life is sometimes. The highway of quick encounters took me to a final destination with no road to ever take me back to where I had started.

I learned virginity is a very personal possession woven in pride, innocence, and love. It's not virginity that's important. Our giving up of our intimate self is greatly intertwined by when, how, where and with whom we share that experience.

CHAPTER 25

TRUE COLORS

The popularity of gay bars in Kansas City shifted as often as the coming of a new moon. The Dover Fox would always remain special in my memory for propelling me into my new world. The Windjammer, a new hotspot located at 20th and Main, occupied an old bank building that dated back to a more thriving era in downtown KC. It attracted a sleazier leather-type crowd with hunky shirtless guys igniting the dance floor with their sexual innuendo.

One evening, the full parking lot next to the building forced me to park across the street from the bar. Crossing busy, four-lane Main Street required careful attention. Misjudging the speed of an oncoming car forced me to stand in the center of the street, waiting for the vehicle to pass. Loud cussing and jeering from a car let me know that they pegged me as a homosexual going into a gay bar. For a second, I feared for my life. I rushed into the bar watching the car that passed. There was a lot of shouting from the windows as it began to slow down. My heart continued pounding even as I reached the service area inside the bar to order a drink.

"Rum and Coke, Mike," I said without my usual hello and smile.

Mike was your typical stereotyped hot, 'nasty,' and muscular bartender. One of those guys to fantasize about and leave a big tip for his sexy smile. "Hey, Jim, buddy. What's wrong? You look like you've just seen a ghost."

Mike grabbed a shot glass and a bottle of premium vodka to pour me a completely full shot. "I'm gonna buy you a drink, Jim. Now, let me teach you how to drink a shot. Don't take sips like I've seen you do. They are meant to be chugged. Grab the glass with your hand shaped like a fist and down it all at once." He leaned over the bar with his hands between the service rails and slapped me on the shoulder and smiled after I downed the vodka. "So, what has you so upset?"

He began to shake his head as I relived my experience, "Jim, you've gotta be more careful. We may be more accepted today than a few years back, but never let your guard down. They could have thrown a bottle at you or even run you down, and they know the cops wouldn't do anything about it. Just forget it for now and have a good time tonight."

Mike's special attention and meeting a hot guy later in the evening washed away the lingering fear and feelings of being hated by so many people in society. Sunday morning was always a day to sleep in to recover from Saturday night. I could never decide if my hangovers were from too much booze, inhaling cigarette smoke all night, or too many "poppers" on the dance floor.

The thing I dreaded most about Mondays and every day of the week was teaching a class called American Problems along with my beloved psychology and geography. Every rookie had to pay their dues by teaching this class for a few years. It was a hard course to teach as it had no textbook. Most kids taking the class didn't like social studies and found it an easy way to earn their one-half unit of the elective social science requirement. Even the negativity of its name contributed to it being a "blow-off" class by students. I tried to enhance the class by running off classroom copies of relevant articles from TIME magazine.

Jerry, a very popular student, never hid his homosexuality. His good-looks, outstanding ability in basketball and quick-wit contributed to his acceptance by everyone. I knew he knew about me though nothing was ever said. His support in anything I tried to accomplish made teaching the ridiculous class easier. Being a gay student or a gay teacher in a very religious and sports-oriented school district could create severe backlash.

A few days before the end of the semester, a very outspoken student critic of the curriculum of my class, Cyndi, was the last to leave the room. Cyndi possessed a crude and rebellious personality. She seemed to switch boyfriends on a daily basis. She sashayed over to my desk to gaze down at my grade book. She ran her fingers along the entire length of the front of my desk.

"I sure need an A in this class," she said.

"Well, Cyndi, you got a B+ at the quarter," I noted as I opened my grade book to check out her progress. "I think doing a good job on your reaction paper on prejudice and discrimination will get you an A for the semester."

"Cool, Mr. R.," she said and smiled as she headed toward the classroom door. Quickly turning around just before leaving the room, she began to tap on her books. "You know, I really need that A. Didn't I see you coming out of one of those funny bars about a month ago on Main Street? We yelled at you, but you just ran into that weird place. I'm sure you wouldn't want that spread around school and what if the principal found out?" Without another word, she disappeared.

I felt like someone had just walked up behind me and slipped a noose around my neck. I quickly rummaged through the reaction papers to read Cyndi's effort.

Please, God, let this be an excellent paper.

It turned out to be one of her typical assignment completions. *Damn little brat. She's playing me and loving every minute of it. What were teenagers from here doing in downtown KC anyway? Should I give up my lifestyle and continue to walk the halls in peace, or let myself be strangled by gossip and tormented by students and staff?*

Two days later, the grade sheets were due by 4 pm. All the grades were bubbled-in except for Cyndi's. I sat at my desk with my No.2 lead pencil looking back and forth at the A and B circles.

I decided to bubble in the B+ she deserved. I laid my head on my desk to ponder the worst outcomes to this scenario. Keeping my head down on the desk, I turned the side of my face toward the open door to my classroom. Then came a tap on the door jam. Surprisingly, it was Jerry. We had never had much communication since I thought that would be revealing my homosexuality.

"Hey, Mr. Rostello. Just thought I'd drop by and let you know not to worry about things with Cyndi. I've taken care of that for you."

"I have no idea what you are talking about," I said quickly.

"What do you mean? I know what's going on. Aren't you going to thank me for working this mess out for you as a fellow friend?"

I quickly grabbed up some papers to grade and walked to the opening of the door. Pulling up a student desk visible to anyone passing in the hall, I began to pretend I was grading a paper. "You got a B in my class for the semester. It's a good improvement."

"Are you kidding me?" Jerry snapped. "Why are you so scared of me and this whole school? Don't you think most everyone knows you are gay and because you are such a good teacher, no one hassles you? And now I try to handle a troublemaker, and you just ignore me?"

"Look, Jerry. You're my student, and I don't want you to fight my battles. It could just make everything worse. I have nothing to say to you about whatever you are talking about."

"There you go again, denying the truth and squelching any friendship."

"I am not here to be your friend, Jerry, I'm your teacher and that's as far as it can go. You know that."

"You know what? I'm really pissed off now," Jerry snarled as he walked over to the wastebasket and opened a piece of gum, throwing the wrapper in the trash before sitting on the edge of my desk. "I've been a little disappointed in you anyway lately. Now I'm really mad. You think that all that matters is what you teach us? Answer me."

"There is nothing I have to say, Jerry."

"Well, I have something to say! I don't understand how you can let three girls from your psychology class come over to your house. You invite them in, give them a drink, and let them smoke in your house. But when two other students who really need a teacher to be a friend come by, you just stand at the door barely talking to them and then let them leave without finding out anything about what was going in their life? You knew one of them. He's a son of a teacher you see every day. He just needed to know that someone can be a successful person and make it in life like you, even though they're gay. And you just turned them away. Are you that scared and in the closet that you let gossip and what people might do keep you from helping a student that needs you?"

"I never let Missy, Rhonda, or Michelle smoke in my house. They went outside to smoke. And I promise you, I would never offer a drink to a student. It would cost me my job. They are girls that have taken several of my classes and so I just let them stay a little while. I don't really feel I owe you any explanation, and I think our conversation is over."

"This is unbelievable," Jerry shouted. "Boy, I really misjudged you. I hope you're happy with your life and okay with only teaching shit that students won't remember anyway when you have the chance to make a difference."

"Jerry, I'm a teacher, not a counselor. They're in a better position to help students."

"You think a straight counselor can do what you could do? You know what? Have it your way, and I hope you can someday accept yourself and be what you really want to be." He turned around and grabbed the name plaque on my desk, turned it upside down, and charged out of the room.

The beautiful name plaque had been made for me by my department chairman at Highland High School. He gave it to me on my first day of teaching. It was octagonal and made of golden-brown rock maple with my name carefully scripted in black.

I walked over to the plate glass windows looking out to a courtyard. A Kansas winter wind tossed small flakes of snow around in the air before they finally made it to the ground. Some would almost hit the ground and then be tossed up in the air again. Some would finally land in the corner of the building. I noticed how green the evergreen shrubs appeared though we were in the grips of winter. No matter how cold or how much snow tried to conceal them, they always found a way to show their true green color.

I wish I could be as strong as those shrubs. They can stand whatever the weather throws at them. Why can't I? Why can't I show my true colors to the world? I guess I'm 100 percent homosexual and not even one percent man.

I walked over to my desk, picked up my name plaque, hurled it into the trash can, and stormed out of the room. All night long, I thought about my first department chairman, how much he helped me, and how I had thrown away that wonderful memory of his influence on my life.

The next morning when I walked into my room, I found my name plaque carefully centered on my desk.

CHAPTER 26

THE BET

A late spring snowstorm warning kept me looking at the back-corner window of my geography classroom. Dark heavy clouds were already spitting huge white flakes quickly dusting the dark green grass of early spring. This usually meant a big storm. We had been reviewing Europe country capitals and country locations.

"Okay, students, tomorrow we'll have the European capitals and locations quiz. The quiz is all matching, just like the Latin America quiz. I know you like the fun activities but you gotta have the basics of geography, too."

"Mr. Rostello," Megan shouted from the back of the room. "We're going to have a snow day tomorrow. We'll study and then we'll have studied for nothing. You've told us the biggest snows in Kansas can be in March."

"Ah, you finally remembered something in this class," I said. "Don't worry, we'll have school tomorrow. The superintendent has used up all of our snow days."

Just then, the principal came on the intercom, "Teachers, you can leave as soon as all the students are out of the building to beat the storm. Drive carefully and listen to morning news for school cancellation. Drive careful."

"Tell you what, students. If we don't have school tomorrow,

I'll give you study time before the quiz on the day we get back."

The students had begun to gather the maps of Europe they had been working on when the classroom door opened a little bit. Tom, an industrial arts teacher, poked his head in the room and snickered, "No school tomorrow! Poker at my house."

"Don't get excited," I snapped. "We'll have school. I don't think this storm will materialize." Tom (Mr. Edwards) let the door shut on its own as he headed back to his classroom.

"You hang out with the jocks and cool teachers, don't you, Mr. Rostello?" Jason asked. "Did you know Mr. Edwards played varsity football at Oklahoma University?"

I always listened to what students said and read between the lines when it came to their comments. They all probably knew I was gay, but I knew it mattered more to their parents. During my 25 years of teaching, my students' attitudes had shifted regarding social attitudes. My students could not understand my interaction with the PE teachers, coaches, and jocks. I was also shocked and proud of their attention. They joked with me, always talked to me in the hall or cafeteria and treated me special. I could tell by Jason's remark and the reaction on my student's faces that my popularity impressed them. The English teachers often told me that students mentioned me in their journals and loved my travel stories, class activities, and antics. I so needed the validation that I was a successful motivator.

Tom was as macho as you could get. Movie star looks, similar to Burt Reynolds, and a build that left nothing to the imagination. More than a few times, I would notice the expression on the female teacher's faces as they passed Tom in the hallway.

Tom meant so much to me. He always defended me as his daughter's best teacher and his friend. He made anything I needed or helped me with man stuff around my house. His spring woodworking show displayed masterpieces from tables to dressers. Tom had a puppy dog nature and was quite the ladies' man, which probably led to his divorce. He had been married for 15 years while his kids were growing up. He remained friends with his ex-wife even after the divorce. Tom's heart and personality matched his face and body, and I always tolerated his corny jokes he told over and over.

Tom charged back into my classroom right after the bell.

"Jimmie, get ready, buddy. We're going to get hit hard. Bring beer to poker."

"Tom, it never snows when it's supposed to, stupid Kansas weather. I bet we don't even get three inches," I challenged.

"Jimmie Joe, you want to make a little bet on that? Say a steak dinner? Your choice of where."

"You're on," I shouted. *Wow, a steak dinner with a hot man. And even if I lose, it's a day off school.*

By the end of last period, the wind had grown stronger, and the snowflakes were smaller and falling more steadily. The principal announced over the intercom that we could leave.

I planned to hit the store to stock up to make a big batch of chili. After I got home and started cooking, I curled up with Chelsea, my dog, to watch the evening weather. The weatherman predicted we were going to get the brunt of the big storm. I looked over to the china cabinet and knew what I should do. I always cleaned it when we were sure to get a snow day.

Being confined to my house gave me the perfect opportunity to really clean the glass shelves, a task I hated.

By 9 p.m., the snow was falling steadily. The news confirmed it was snowing heavily in Lawrence, a city 40 miles to the west. I fixed a vodka tonic, and then several more. I turned up the stereo and began working on the china cabinet, a big job I hated. I always removed all the inlaid glass from the doors to get it perfectly clean. By 2 a.m. I had finished drying the crystal to put back in the cabinet. The music and all the vodka had kept me from checking on the status of the storm.

My dog, Chelsea, wandered into the dining room from a long sleep on the bed to go outside. When I opened the door to let her out, I discovered it had stopped snowing with barely two or three inches on the porch.

"Oh my God, shit, fuck! The snow is over." I stormed outside in my fuzzy slippers to see a star-filled sky. Chelsea just looked at me as I crazily ranted at the cloudless sky. "Fucking Kansas weather. Now I have to get up in just a few hours and go to school. That's barely enough time for me to get sober!"

I stumbled into school that morning hungover and mad. The only consolation would be the steak dinner.

Tom stood, waiting in front of my classroom door. "You lucky little shit. I'll pick you up Saturday around 6 p.m."

The steak dinner tasted great and the view was even better. Tom kept ordering us beer after beer along with tequila shots. His conversation centered on fucking. "Are you getting regular pussy?" he asked as his eyes glistened.

"I get it all the time. You know us Italians," I assured him.

"Hmmm, do you like three ways? Know a gal that would party with us?" Tom was on the prowl. "Let's go to your house and see what we can find." My bluff had been called.

"Yeah, I have a girlfriend that might do it. Her name's Big Red."

"Wow," Tom's eyes twinkled as he quickly paid the bill for dinner. "Let's go to your place right now and call her."

We headed to my house, talking about hot sex the whole time. Tom especially liked hearing about Big Red's tits and oral expertise.

"Can she take care of us both," my buddy asked. He squirmed in his seat.

My lies were getting me deeper in trouble. I now needed to find a way out. The minute we got to my house, Tom went to my phone and handed me the receiver.

"Don't fuck up now, stud. Be cool." He pulled out a joint to light up and handed it to me. "This might help."

I dialed a fake number and handed the joint back to him. While he enjoyed a long hit, I pushed down the receiver button on the phone to end the call without him noticing.

"She's not home," I said, acting disappointed.

Suddenly, I felt Tom's hands around my crotch. I couldn't believe it.

"Want to mess around?" He whispered, playing with my

crotch while putting his other hand on my ass.

"Sounds good to me," I quickly agreed, reaching for his bulge.

Tom followed me to my bedroom. By the time I lit a candle, he was already naked, lying on my bed. He hadn't been wearing any underwear under his jeans. He reached over and unleashed my belt and began to unzip me. This was a dream too good to be true, maybe too good. As I jumped on the bed between his legs, I could not believe the sight. His equipment was beer-can thick and unbelievably long. I had never seen anything like it. I knew I better not try kissing him, so I tried to go down on him, but to no avail. I couldn't handle it. Then his hand under me told me what he really wanted. As much as I desired to do that, there was no way that it would fit where he had in mind. *Damn, what do I do? Throw it over my shoulder and burp it? No matter how much I wanted to do what he needed, it just wasn't going to happen.*

I could see Tom becoming impatient and disappointed, knowing I couldn't do what he had in mind.

"Guess I should stick with girls. They don't seem to have as much trouble as you do. You are my buddy, though. You know I love you, Jimmie. Want to just lay down next to me and hold each other?"

Sex was no longer the most important thing on my mind. Now it was the wonderful satisfaction just holding and cuddling with that fantastic man. I surrendered to his embrace, to his manhood. I finally fell asleep lost in space and time. The sound of the front door shutting woke me up. He had slipped away during the night, and that part of our relationship ended forever.

While in his forties, Tom divorced his wife. He eventually remarried a wonderful person and the three of us were best friends. We took weekend trips together and talked several times a day at school. We often went out to eat and drink together. Though she knew everything that had happened between me and Tom, she never said anything. Tom took early retirement at the age of 55 to enjoy his newfound happiness. With another year to go, I anxiously awaited my own retirement when I would finally be able to move to San Diego.

During the first week of May, a knock came at my classroom door during fifth period.

Tom must want to take me out for a beer after school, I thought.

When I opened the door, the attendance secretary was staring at me with a shocked look on her face. I quickly assured her the attendance slip had been turned in.

"Jim, I just heard from Tom's first wife. Something's happened to Tom, and it's not good."

My best friend had died, and I never knew how. His current wife secluded herself from everyone.

He had always protected me and helped me with anything I asked. He liked me for my personality. His friendship was unconditional. He had a history of getting the good-looking ladies, but chose a wonderful and beautiful woman who loved doing activities they both enjoyed and could do together. Today, Tom's looks and body are not what I treasure about his friendship.

There is a neighborhood called Strawberry Hill on the western banks of the Kansas River in Kansas City. Settlers from Croatia found prolific wild strawberries flourishing there. Though small in size, the berries were sweet and abundant. They soon disappeared with the coming of settlement. Tom was like those strawberries, never meant to be fenced and harnessed by the barbed wire social mores.

CHAPTER 27

NO GLOVE, NO LOVE

"Jim, kiss me," Laura whispered as her lips drew close to mine. I couldn't believe what I had just heard. I felt so proud to be wanted by a beautiful straight woman. Laura had been in Broadway musicals, had been a TV news anchor in a major market, and now was an English and film studies teacher at Olathe High. Her soft blonde hair and pale blue eyes adorned a perfect complexion and beautiful face. *What did she see in me? I'm a gay man, not even above average in looks, and an underpaid schoolteacher.*

I moved closer to Laura as we scooted to the edge of the steps in the dark stairway leading into the little theater. We often met there over lunch break at school to tell each other everything we couldn't tell anyone else.

"Oh, Laura, yes, yes, I want to kiss you." It became a moment I had imagined in a dream: I was a straight man being sought after by a gorgeous woman. Our lips met slowly and carefully. Her eyes closed a second before mine. Our kiss created a spiraling sensation in me not manifested by sexual urge, but rather a fulfillment of everything I wished could happen in life.

We held each other's hands as our lips parted.

"Jim, I so wish things could have been different between us. I'm now on my fifth husband, and his youth and looks haven't changed anything in my life. I just can't find what I'm looking for…I don't know what I'm trying to find. That's the scary part. I think you could've been my companion even though I know we could never really be together because you're gay. But I do love you. Love is still love regardless of whether or not two people can be together, don't you think?"

"Oh, yes. You're my special friend, a friend beyond friendship." I looked down to the stage in the mostly darkened theater. *Why can't my life be like a play where anything can be and anything can happen?*

"Jim, will you promise me something?" Laura pleaded softly. "Olathe is not for me. I'm going to be leaving this year or next. I'm worried about something and want you to be careful. I just heard about this new disease in the gay community. With it, death is painful and swift and it's going around New York and San Francisco right now. The Department of Health says it will be a mass killer and will change the world forever. They don't even know what's causing it. Please be careful."

"I have no idea what you are talking about. I'll be careful if it comes to Kansas City. It won't though. Things are safer here."

Laura and I held each other, but did not kiss a second time. There was nothing more to reveal. She left Olathe the following year after getting divorced again. We lost touch immediately. Our relationship was best left as a memory and a wish.

Within a year of Laura leaving Olathe, came the news of a rapidly spreading virus among homosexuals in almost every major U.S. city. A suspect Canadian flight attendant had infected a multitude of partners. The disease was similar to a virus in Africa stemming from a possible mutation transferred from monkeys to humans. The disease was transmissible through blood transfusions and the exchange of a wide range of bodily fluids. Condoms became the most successful deterrent to catching the disease through sex. President Reagan refused to sign emergency research funding, saying it would not affect heterosexuals.

Being strong-willed, I immediately adopted a "no glove, no love" policy. No matter how cute or how much more fun 'bareback' sex could be, I never played it unsafe. Some of my friends laughed or questioned my paranoia until they were given death sentences from AIDS.

In 1981, I met and fell for a guy named Mitch. He was special, and although I wanted an exclusive relationship with him; he did not feel the same. A friend of mine had seen him at the bathhouse in Kansas City, but as they say, love is blind. I just knew that he would settle down with me. He did not want to practice safe sex, and I began to ponder ending my strict condom code. Luckily, given his personal endowment, our sex was primarily oral; I knew a decision had to be made about giving him what he wanted in order to keep him in my life.

• • •

Always striving to be the best I could be at anything I did, I knew traveling the world would help me become an exciting geography teacher. Sharing travel experiences and having interesting slides would mean so much more to my students than just memorizing the capitals and products of countries. On a trip to England, I distracted the guard at the Tower of London and walked away with slides of the Crown Jewels: an unheard-of feat. Getting that one and only photo that became slides for the classroom became my travel obsession.

I decided to take a trip around the world in the summer of 1981. Pan Am airlines was selling a one-way ticket with unlimited stops for $1200 as long as the journey continued in the same direction until you circled the world and returned to your departure city. With a summer break of eighty-five days and $5000 for my expenses, I vowed to do it all.

I fell deeper and deeper in love with Mitch, I contemplated canceling my trip. Wondering if I would lose him if I left for that length of time, I turned to Rita for advice. She was a fellow social studies teacher and good friend.

She discouraged me from cancelling the trip. "Jim, staying home will put too much pressure on you and him and the relationship, and, if this thing between you and Mitch is meant to be and he really cares for you, he'll be there when you get back."

Knowing she was right, I accepted that I probably cared more for him than he did for me. By my return, he had moved on. Luckily, because I worried about my getting too involved before leaving, I had resisted being the bottom guy in anal intercourse.

I reveled in being featured in a Kansas City Star and Times article that brought accolades to my school district. I had seen the Taj Mahal under moonlight, climbed to the top of Ayers Rock in Australia's outback, and wandered forbidden streets in Red China. I had carefully recorded unbelievable experiences in my daily journal with corresponding slides. Geography came alive for my students. The trip also mellowed my self-pity on my life as a homosexual. I learned that people all over the world suffer prejudice and struggle with many different aspects of living. The most important thing about my adventure: it probably saved my life. Mitch became sick a short time after I returned home. Traveling and not consummating anal sex with Mitch probably saved me from AIDS.

Through the 1980s and 1990s friend after friend died, keeping me firm on my commitment to safe sex.

CHAPTER 28

MY FAVORITE MOVIE

By the time I turned 31 in 1980, I was living as a gay man in my private life though I remained in the closet publicly. My job, respect from students, and my day-to-day interactions with others had to be protected. Knowing I would never have children or a marriage partner weighed heavy on my heart.

I believe that when you are honest with yourself and your students instead of being someone you are not, you foster respect and empathy. As the teacher, you have to keep certain beliefs and thoughts private. I would never talk outside the realm of my subject and never share conflicting values. However, when communicating and dealing with a student, you have to be yourself.

• • •

Mandy always managed to ruin a teacher's day. To make matters worse, she was the daughter of a good teacher. It's hard to tell a colleague that their child is a pain in the ass and to try and get them to act somewhat like a normal child.

One day, the minute Mandy walked into my class, I knew she had chosen me as her target. Every encouragement to just work on her geography map assignment and be quiet incited her to even worse behavior. Finally, she gathered her belongings to storm out the door. As she pushed the automatically closing door to slam it, she screamed, "Mr. Rostello, why don't you just GO TO HELL!"

"I'll see you there," I shouted back to her.

The next day as she passed my desk, she leaned over to me and with a smile said, "You are a hell of a guy, you said exactly what I needed to hear. I like your spunk and telling it like it is."

She never gave me any real trouble after that. She worked in the bakery section at the grocery store where I shopped, and with every Danish I ordered, she would throw in an extra one. I gladly took advantage of her new appreciation of me.

• • •

Our school district had a closed lunch policy. Students often complained they could not go to McDonald's for lunch. Of course, some parents wanted their little darlings to have everything they want in life.

One semester, I had lunchroom duty. Toward the end of a lunch time, in came a parent bringing slabs of ribs for their child's entire table. The kids devoured them like lions eating a wildebeest. I noticed the custodian surveying the mess, knowing he would have to clean it up. The bell rang, and sure enough, they started to dart off to class leaving behind the carnage.

Motioning and pointing at the table, I screamed, "Pick up the fucking rib bones. The janitor should not have to clean up your mess." With my supervision, they mumbled and grumbled as they cleaned off the table.

About halfway down the hall as I walked to my classroom, the following announcement came on the all-call intercom, "Will Mr. Rostello please report immediately to the principal's office?" The principal, surrounded by assistants, asked me if I told some students to pick up their mess by using the F-word. I said, "It's okay to put in my file that I said pick up the fucking rib bones." Everyone started laughing. "We can all read this now and then reread it when I retire in a few years."

• • •

One girl in my class constantly refused to work and talked anytime she felt like it. She was downright hateful. At parent-teacher conferences, I asked her mom in attendance to please ask her to be more polite and accommodating. Her mother responded, "My daughter doesn't get along with you or her father either but that is okay. I am my daughter's best friend. I even bought her a dress that cost over 500 dollars and I didn't even tell her father and it was just our secret. I won't tell him about this conference either."

I responded, "Well, I am your daughter's teacher, not her best friend. Daughters have lots of friends, but only one mother." I really caught hell for that one.

• • •

Teaching geography and psychology at a large high school fulfilled my teaching aspirations. I always demanded exactness on map assignments, and students often said my tests were the hardest. However, cultivating student interest in the subject of geography and making it alive and fun for them was top priority for me. I created games like "Geography Feud," adapted from the TV game show Family Feud.

By the late '70s, I was traveling around the United States, Europe, and the world. I made my slides into synchronized shows using a sync recorder and slide projector. Students marveled at my slides of blood dripping from a cheetah's mouth as he devoured the gazelle he had caught. The safari guide had said I was lucky to see the cheetah eyeing his prey, chasing it, and conquering it all in one. Life was simpler then, and students still enjoyed and were interested in simple travel slides. I always stressed the importance of world culture and its presence in our everyday lives. For example, in those days, a handshake was still legally binding in The Netherlands, its country of origin.

I also believed that students needed to have some fun, too. Every student had heard of the "Rostello Shuffle" and asked about it every day until it came time for my lesson on climate.

"Okay, students. Today, I'm going to show you how knowing the different climates in the United States can help you meet the girl of your dreams. Let's say, guys, that you're 22 and it's a Friday after a long work week. It's happy hour at the bar, and you see the girl of your dreams. You can't just charge over to her and fall at her feet. You have to ease your way over to her side as if it were destiny. Girls are really into meant-to-be and chance meetings. So now you use the 'Rostello Shuffle.'"

From the middle of the classroom, I unleashed a series of sideways turns and shuffles and backward turns until I ended up next to the large black filing cabinet on the side of the room. By this time, the students were hanging over the tops of the desks and giggling.

"See, guys, you've now positioned yourself next to her, and a simple thing like knowing the climates of the U. S. can help you make the next move." I began to role-play, playing both the guy and girl, jumping from one side of the file cabinet to the other to indicate character changes.

"Hi, how are you?"

"I'm fine."

"I'm Jim. I haven't seen you before. Are you from here?"

"Not really. I just moved here for a new job. I'm from Seattle. Oh, I'm Melanie."

"Ah, Seattle. Don't you miss the misty nights and mornings just along the Puget Sound and down the coast all the way to San Francisco? Everything is so green, but the rains are gentle. It's never cold even though just 100 miles away you have beautiful snow-capped mountains most of the year. I love the way the leaf-bearing trees are back-dropped by evergreens of the mixed forests in fall. The color contrasts are beautiful."

"Oh, yes. I love the coast and the wonderful weather it creates. I don't know if I'll ever get used to Kansas City."

"You will. It's hot and humid in the summer and cold in the

winter, but it'll grow on you. Being in the middle of the country, we have that humid continental climate that makes all four seasons romantic. Tell you what; let's go to my place. It's cold out tonight. I'll build a big fire in the fireplace, and we can talk about all the wonderful things about Seattle."

"Sure, do you make a good nightcap?"

I ended the role-play with the following scenario:

"See there, students, knowing your geography can help you be successful in life. Now, let's go over the rest of the characteristics of American climates. There will be a quiz on them tomorrow." Though it took a little settling down, the students were always easier to work with after a little controlled fun in the classroom.

I loved teaching psychology as much as geography. I learned quickly that teaching the dynamics of behavior to 17 and 18 year-old students was as difficult as teaching any math or science class. The concepts of conscious, preconscious, and unconscious; the difference between negative reinforcement and punishment; and such things as how a person could be acquitted of murder due to temporary insanity were just a few of the many challenging concepts I had to teach.

Teaching in a conservative environment was also difficult. I remained strong in teaching the fundamentals of psychology though faced with illogical barriers. I could see that understanding psychology made a difference in life. Counselors encouraged me to keep up the good work, telling me that some students who'd signed up for my class asked not to let their parents know until after the window to change class schedules had closed. Some parents went to the school board to stop me from teaching meditation even though the textbook used valid research to support its benefits. Some claimed that mantras took people's focus from God and represented the Anti-Christ.

One technique I used in my psychology classes was the song "Games People Play," which was a popular alternative song. Through its lyrics, it taught the understanding of self, optimal behavior, and the danger of always using defense mechanisms in life. One line warned listeners that some people used identification with God to cheat others, "People walking up to you singing Glory, Hallelujah and they try to sock it to you in the name of the Lord."

One day, after I had played the record and assigned students to interpret the song, a student shouted out, "You have committed blasphemy and you are possessed by the devil."

My students taught me an important lesson that day. Many class members just looked away and shook their heads, but did not confront him. Instead of being my usual confrontational self, I just gazed out at the class and continued teaching. I took the lead of my students.

My early years of teaching in Olathe, Kansas, drove me deeper and deeper into the closet. For a time, I dared not mention the newest scientific research that indicated that homosexuality was organically, not functionally, caused. Even mentioning homosexuality would have had negative consequences. Eventually, when I addressed heredity's role in behavior, several ministers demanded to have equal time in the classroom. They wanted to let my classes know that all behavior is a choice, and that God can change these choices if you pray to Him and believe in His power. Kansas even made national news when the state legislature supported a law that required creationism be taught alongside evolution in science classes. Even though most of the students I taught at my first teaching job at Highland High School had attended church, I had never experienced more conservative views than I did in Kansas.

Mr. Williamson's theories elevated psychology to a very empathic and powerful way to understand behavior. His phenomenological concepts could change lives and personal interactions if successfully applied, but executing effective classroom instruction of his concepts and related behaviors were difficult in both the high school and college levels. Role-playing, experiments, and other techniques were helpful but often did not lead to a true understanding of behavior or behavioral changes. Practicing as well as knowing is difficult in psychology. It was hard for me to personally recognize that I unconsciously sabotaged most of the relationships in my life but blamed it on other things, not myself. I knew that somehow, I needed students to see the importance of psychology in life demonstrated in realistic ways. Educational videos helped explain psychological concepts.

One evening, I met a friendly guy standing near the dance floor. During our conversation, I found out he had a good job and lived in North Kansas City. I went back to his place with him and had a great time in bed. I enjoyed staying all night and having good conversation after the sex. He asked me if I wanted to see a movie the following weekend. I agreed, thinking that surely no one from southwestern Olathe would be at a movie theater in North KC.

The movie turned out to be Ordinary People starring Mary Tyler Moore, which was about a teenager's struggles. That movie became an integral part of my teaching career and my life. Every scene in the movie exhibited one of Mr. Williamson's theories in ways my students could relate to in that it was about teen life and dysfunctional family. All the theories of psychology were put into action through this movie. The movie exhausted me, and I actually could not concentrate on anything else when it was over. I just went home instead of staying the night with my new friend. We never got together again.

Luckily, I had a buddy in California who was a film hobbyist, and he was able to come up with a copy of the movie on tape. He was even able to remove the cursing. I had never thought of showing a movie in class as a teaching strategy before. Most movies took too much time and always had parts not related to the topic of discussion. Some teachers showed movies once in a while before holidays. My students quickly realized when I passed out the study guide that accompanied the movie that it was not going to be free class time.

The movie begins with Conrad, a high school student, waking up from a recurring nightmare of his brother's drowning that had happened during a forbidden outing on the family sailboat when it was storming. Conrad survives, and his mother, Beth (played by Mary Tyler Moore), blames him for the death of her firstborn son, Bucky. Conrad has just been released from a mental hospital after attempting suicide. The movie centers on Conrad losing his mother's recognition and care. Mr. Williamson had always stressed that love and recognition from significant others are essential for fostering self-esteem and feelings of security that get us through good and bad times in our lives.

The movie portrays this in a myriad of events including one scene where the father wants to take a picture of Conrad and his mother at a Thanksgiving Dinner. The mother begins suggesting other photo ops and insisting the father give her the camera. Conrad screams at him: "Give her the Goddamn camera," perceiving his mother doesn't want to even stand next to him.

The father insists on Conrad seeing a psychiatrist after being released from the mental hospital. The psychiatrist believes in client-centered therapy. My instruction focused on Gestalt psychology with an emphasis on empathy and letting the patient discover how to deal with their life. There are continuous revelations of these principles throughout the movie. Even at the beginning, the psychiatrist forces Conrad to decide if he is willing to give the time for therapy and juggle it with swimming practice. It makes Conrad mad and frustrated—he even demands that the doctor tell him what to do since it is the doctor's job to know best—but eventually chooses to continue therapy. By getting mad, Conrad shows that implosive therapy is sometimes needed to bring a person's feelings to the conscious level, which can be a cure.

At one point, Conrad reaches out to a girl named Karen who had been in the same psychiatric ward as him, where psychotropic pills were used as a cure. While meeting for a burger, she tells Conrad that he must try to live in reality. She says that her life is good, and she is in a school play. She doesn't miss fellow patients like Conrad does. Karen encourages Conrad to get out and live in the real world and ends by saying, "That's what my father says."

In choir, Conrad meets a girl name Jenine. She is not the typical girl who just wants a date. They begin to get close and Conrad gains significant female recognition in his life though his mother continues to reject him. The father is caught in the middle. The movie highlights so many important phenomenological theories.

Because he and his brother had had the same circle of friends, Conrad struggles with being around many of their friends. Of course, there is one that makes fun of him for being in the mental hospital. One night while Conrad and Jenine are having a Coke at the drugstore after a bowling date, they finally discuss their feelings and life. She looks at the scar on his wrist and asks him about it. Amazingly, Conrad begins to describe the hole that depression created in his mental health and how it kept getting bigger and bigger until it swallowed him up.

At the worst possible moment, several friends of Conrad and his deceased brother drunkenly stumble into the drugstore. One takes his hat off and puts it on Jenine, and everyone except Conrad laughs. Jenine is innocently forced into being social and joking around with them. Mr. Williamson always stressed the importance of realistic and accurate perceptions for our behavior to be optimal. Conrad misinterprets the interaction and thinks Jenine does not really appreciate how he has opened up to her. He immediately shuts down and takes her home without another word.

He ends up going to the school gym. A shallow friend walks up to him and asks if he had gotten into Jenine's pants yet. That triggers Conrad's instability, and he begins attacking the guy. It takes several people to pull him off.

He finally gets to his grandmother's house, disoriented and roaming around until after midnight. He was staying there because his mother had talked the father into a golfing trip without Conrad. Conrad decides to reach out to Karen, his friend from the mental hospital. When he arouses Karen's father from sleep, the father stutters and then answers in disorientation: "Karen is dead. She killed herself."

Conrad runs to the bathroom, locks the door, and begins to run cold water over his wrist to numb the pain. He then starts to slash his left wrist like the previous time. But his situation is now different because of Jenine and his psychiatrist. He throws the knife down and calls the doctor and asks him to meet him. It is now after midnight, but the doctor goes to his office to be there for Conrad. Conrad is so disoriented from the trauma that he can hardly make it to the doctor's office. The doctor went to the office to be there for him. Because Conrad's defenses are down, the doctor is able to get to his subconscious. While disoriented, Conrad is guided into a role-play by the doctor. The doctor pretends to be the drowning brother at the moment the boat capsized. Conrad screams for him to hang onto the boat. The psychiatrist pretends to be Bucky and drowns by letting go. Now the doctor can instill in Conrad that he isn't responsible for Bucky's death. The doctor reminds Conrad that he hung onto the boat and survived and "surely you can live with that."

Through client-centered psychotherapy, Conrad can now see that he is a worthwhile person. Jenine cares about him, his father cares about him, and, most importantly, he can now realistically perceive himself and others.

He goes to Jenine's house the next morning after leaving the doctor's office. He stands there until she sees him outside. When she comes out, he apologizes for overreacting when she was just having fun with the other guys who interrupted their date. He confesses to having done many dumb things recently. Jenine apologizes for her reaction to the situation as well. Then, Conrad admits he wrongly thought that she didn't care about him.

Conrad looks at her affectionately and says: "I want to try again. I think our dating worked." Jenine agrees.

Now Conrad has accurate perceptions of reality and can make the right choices. Conrad's behavior is no longer determined by low self-concept stemming from his mother's rejection. His willingness to go back to Jenine the next morning, after his psychiatrist's intervention, shows the strength of his recovery. When his parents return, he goes up to his mother to hug her. She freezes in place with no response. The father observes this and begins to question his love for her given where things have gone in the family. She leaves, and Conrad sees his father sitting alone after watching his mother get into a cab to leave. He goes outside and begins to blame himself for her leaving, but his father immediately convinces him that it wasn't his fault. They have a man-to-man talk about life, and Conrad is able to respond and even tells his father that he loves him.

The movie "Ordinary People" remained an important part of my teaching until I retired in 2005. Neither the outdated cars or clothes or signs of the time affected the power of the movie. Rather, it centered more on personal changes and the examination of behavior, and it did not seem to date itself. Events like the fight that Conrad had with the immature friend who asked if he was sleeping with Jenine were relevant as this is what kids still do today. Everyone can understand and relate to mother and son or father and son relationships.

As I approached the end of my teaching career, I wondered: *Did this movie make a difference?* I hoped it had over all the years.

I once wrote to my niece questioning why my mother and uncle had difficulties getting along. It seemed our extended family fought all the time. She said she did not know the reason, but she gave me this wonderful insight, "Jim, you can't really understand a problem unless you're part of it."

I always tried to show my personality to my students through doing silly little things like singing Tina Turner songs or talking about my life and its dependence on psychology. Over the years, came the joy of students keeping in touch with me and their brothers or sisters wanting to take my class. Because their sibling had been in my class, I came to believe that being unconventional was a gift in my teaching.

CHAPTER 29

LOVE AT FIRST SIGHT

Throughout the 1990s and up until 2005, I dreamed of an early retirement, though being fully engaged with my students and teaching. Besides creative techniques in geography and psychology, I sponsored several clubs and organizations. Not wanting National Honor Society students to be recognized only for their academic performance, I required community service. Students felt it changed their perspective on life and what is important.

My biggest goal in life was retiring to San Diego. Once I became invested in spending several years of teaching experience in Kansas, moving to California would have meant a big cut in salary. Transferring steps on the salary scale were limited to a certain number of years depending on the state. From childhood, moving to the Golden State had been my dream. Though considered a top candidate for a teaching job in Escondido, California, after my graduation, my not being bilingual took me out of the competition.

Every year, no matter how busy, I would spend several weeks in San Diego. Becoming more spiritual left me believing in reincarnation. It felt like home. Finally accepting my homosexuality, California offered more acceptance of people and lifestyles. Whenever San Francisco was mentioned in geography

191

class in Olathe, students mumbled and denounced "faggots."

Using my house design and decorating skills brought great financial success, permitting me to move to an expensive state. Fellow teachers would sneer at my goal to leave Kansas. Some predicted I would not last in California and return to Kansas City. Even close friends would tease me about moving to the land of fruits, flakes, and nuts, but in 2005, I bought a small, but cute single-family home in San Diego, California. I treated myself to professional movers and left Kansas in January with my schnauzer, dropping off my winter coat at a 7-Eleven on my way out of town.

I took retirement seriously; I had no desire to work. I felt free to display the LGBT rainbow flag on my porch and walk hand-in-hand with a date. Just hanging out in a neighborhood called Hillcrest brought such joy. Working so hard in Olathe, Kansas, had left no time for my hobby of bowling. With no job to protect, I joined a gay bowling league. My good bowling average quickly returned to the high 180s, and I found that some gay bowlers were among the best in SD.

A retired Marine organized a gay bowling league on the military base, and he approved the league and gave us a military discount. A few Marines joined. After a few weeks, the General found out about the league. He cancelled our league with no option to even finish the season. We heard his comment was, "I will not have my boys subjected to having queers on base." My personal life had continued to follow me; just like Mom said the day the hobo came to our backdoor.

I desperately desired to be openly gay in my everyday life, especially when doing the things I enjoyed. Bowling had always been my passion and being on a gay league was a dream come true. I quickly became disillusioned. A person being cute or having the highest bowling average would cause constant shifting in teams and dictated who bowled with whom in tournaments. Straight leagues were more about bowling, and backstabbing did not exist.

Shortly after getting settled in California, I lost my schnauzer, Chelsea. She was 16 years old. At least she had made it to San Diego with me. I dated a few guys, but relationships didn't materialize.

Being 56 narrowed my dating options. Most relationship-oriented guys were already with someone. The fact that so many people around my age had died of AIDS also limited the number of available guys. I worked hard to convince myself that my financial security in my golden years could bring happiness without a lover in my life.

By 2006, there were many online dating sites. They offered a whole new world for meeting people. You could survey online profiles and meet people without ever stepping foot in a bar. One evening, while I was checking out guys online, I received an interesting e-mail in the chat room. At only 32, Joel quickly let me know that he liked mature guys and encouraged me not to rule him out because of our 20-year age difference. His photo showed that he was extremely handsome and had a great physique. His profile indicated maturity. We decided to meet at my house with "no-strings" expectations. I agreed with him that meeting someone in their home revealed a lot about their personality.

When he appeared at my door, my heart must have skipped a thousand beats. His coarse, black Irish hair and intense brown eyes were stunning. He exceeded all of my expectations.

When I sat down, he jumped up from the sofa to join me on the loveseat. His navy blue checked shirt brushed my arm. My initial feelings were beyond description. His looks and youth captivated me from the first moment we met. I hung on his every word about his college football days and what he wanted in life. He seemed well on his way to achieving his goals. I thought about the many times I told my psychology students that there was no such thing as love at first sight. Real love had to develop like a giant skyscraper being slowly built to reach the sky. I wanted young teens to be careful about moving too fast too quickly.

Wow, I love this guy, and we've just met. What's going on with me? I can't understand these sudden overwhelming feelings. Please God, let him love me, too.

In a dream come true, Joel turned to me, held me close to him, and whispered in my ear, "Jim, you are exactly the kind of guy I'm looking for. I think we're going to have a lot of great times together."

With that, I became a believer in love at first sight.

After a few drinks and a lot of talking and laughter, Joel suggested that we could have some fun. He would be mine for the night if I wanted. He asked if we could spend a little time in my hot tub, and, of course, that sounded great to me. As we stripped down before heading out to the jacuzzi, I couldn't believe my eyes. *How could this handsome, intelligent, fantastically built hunk of guy be gifted in so many ways except in the most personal of attributes?* Always being somewhat of a "size-queen," I couldn't believe my eyes; he had certainly misrepresented that particular aspect of himself in his profile. Amazingly, in the end, it didn't matter. His personality, his looks, and the way he treated me all meant more than his size. That feeling proved to me that I loved this guy.

"Jim, I just broke up with a guy I'd been dating because of his infidelity. That's why I came to meet you this evening. A couple of months ago, I found out that he actually went to sex clubs and gave me a little present from his escapades. Can you believe it? How do you feel about fooling around when you are seeing someone on a regular basis?"

"Joel, I don't do sex clubs. And if I meet a great guy, I'm usually exclusive after just a couple of dates."

"Jim, I think we'll go far."

It felt so good for Joel to spend the night. Most guys just wanted to have fun and then leave. Finally, around 5:00 a.m., my new dreamboat left to tend to his dog before going to work. We made plans for the weekdays because he would not have to go out of town with his part-time rock band. A "rocker" was rocking my world.

He always let me know when he had to work and, therefore, was unable to make it over on evenings we had planned to be together. We usually saw each other at least once a week, but his job kept him extremely busy. For our first Valentine's Day dinner, I fixed my traditional spaghetti and meatballs. As we relaxed in the hot tub, I asked him about his home, which he'd often told me about.

"I want to have you over so bad and show you that I'm a great cook," he laughed. "I wish I had my own home instead of buying a house with a guy I work with to fix up and resell. He's very religious like all the guys at my company. My CEO is a big member of the Nazarene Church in University City. Having a guy over for dinner would cause everyone to talk."

"You're so damn right," I said. "Olathe is home to the Nazarenes, and teaching psychology there was always a hassle. Parents didn't even want me to really teach all aspects of psychology."

Joel shook his head in agreement. "Tell you what, Jim. You talk about how much you love New England. My parents have a cabin there and we should go sometime. There's a recipe for wild blueberry muffins tacked to the bulletin board in the kitchen. I'll cook for you, and we can have a great getaway."

I checked airfares the next day, and Joel promised he would free up some time when he could. He encouraged me to be patient because his career was starting to take off and he needed to establish his job security. Often during the evenings with me, he would have to step outside and take cell phone calls to deal with some problem with his job. There never seemed to be enough time to get out and do all the things we wanted to do. He claimed to be a 200 average bowler and that he would beat my butt as soon as he had some free time and was not too tired from working all day. Just to get out and bowl a few games always seemed impossible. My God, when I was his age, I could work all day and play all night.

The more I drew closer to him and needed him emotionally, the more he seemed to worry about what he could give me. I assured him that my being retired did not mean that I didn't realize he had to work and only had so much time for us. One night he arrived at my house later than scheduled. I felt selfish regarding our limited time together and began to question him about arriving so late in the evening. I was trying hard to be understanding about Joel's attempts to balance new love and a demanding job. When I tried to kiss him to make up, I felt rejection and withholding in his kiss. The emotional pain of that rejected kiss gave me one of the worst feelings I've ever experienced in my life.

"I'm just so worried I can't be what you need right now, Jim. Maybe I'm not right for you."

The next day he called me and told me how much he cared and that he didn't want to stop seeing me. I shared my ongoing concerns with Sharon, a neighbor and close friend. She was always able to predict relationship outcomes, and she assured me that I was winning him over and should be patient. Joel wanted to bring all the ingredients to make dinner for me the following Saturday night. When I met him at the door to help carry in groceries, I noticed that he had driven a Mustang to my house rather than his Toyota Corolla.

"Wow, so you own two cars, Joel? How can you afford that?" Joel just laughed. He said the car belonged to his roommate, and he drove it because it had been parked behind his car in the driveway. It really didn't matter to me what he drove. I still loved him.

After a couple of months, our times together were mostly evenings when there was time for him to swing by. His work, band, and house projects kept him busy and tired. We still had not gone bowling or out and about to just enjoy a day.

Finally, Sharon asked why she had never met Joel or seen him around much during the day. Then she asked, "Have you and Joel ever gone anywhere?" She knew I had completely fallen for him. She became concerned about the limited time we had together. It seemed like we only got together to have dinner and sex at my house.

"Jim, I want you to do me a favor," Sharon said. "Make a definite time with Joel to go bowling or out to eat and see if that really happens. I think there is something not right with you and Joel."

Quickly defending our relationship, I assured her that everything would work out and I became determined to give him the time he needed.

As it happened, the next night before I was getting ready to leave for a bowling tournament in Phoenix, Joel was supposed to come over to spend some time with me. We were going to meet for a bite to eat and then go to my place. I would be gone for a week and counted so much on seeing him before I left. As much as I loved gay bowling tournaments, I would miss him deeply. My life revolved around a romance that had grown fast yet strong.

Joel called from his office around 3:00 p.m. "Hey, Jim. Really crazy day at work today. I'm beat. How about a splash in the Jacuzzi? I'll bring a pizza from Bronx Pizza."

"Of course," I said understandingly. "Around 7:00, though, I need to run to the bowling alley pro shop and have the thumb hole made bigger in my bowling ball before leaving tomorrow. The guy that drills bowling balls won't be there until the leagues have started. You can come inside with me and I'll buy you a beer while I get the ball fixed."

"No, Jim. Didn't you hear what I just said to you? I'm tired and not up to going out once I get to your place."

"It won't even take 15 minutes," I explained. "I've got to get this ball fixed before heading out of town for this big tournament." There was silence on the phone. "Are you there," I asked.

"Well, I guess you have made your decision," Joel responded. "If your bowling ball is that important, then you take care of that, and maybe we can get together when you get back."

His voice sounded so stern and cold that I felt rejection and a chilling lack of love from him.

"I've got to go now," Joel quickly snapped and hung up.

I ran to my neighbor's house in a state of shock and fear. Sharon lowered the boom on me by sternly prophesying that Joel was a married man. She advised me to get on my computer and go to a people finder site and spend $39 to find out the details I needed to know. I didn't have the courage to do that until after Joel and I broke up.

I didn't want to accept the facts about our relationship. I knew my neighbor had to be right. Never going out in public was not the only red flag she recognized. Yet I grasped at one more speck of hope that he was being true to me. "Sharon, he's stayed all night with me several times," I said, defending the relationship.

"How could he be married and stay all night?"

"Jim, his wife could be a nurse or something. I just don't want you to face a woman with a child in hand at your door someday asking you what's going on between you and her husband. You're a man of integrity, Jim. I know you'll do the right thing here."

While traveling with my bowling friend across the desert to the Phoenix tournament, I cried relentlessly. Joel didn't respond to any of the voicemails I left him for the next two days. Finally, he left me an email saying we could talk later. I proceeded to write a ridiculously long email in which I took all of the blame for our problems and prostrated myself at his mercy. And then I received the dreaded reply. His "Dear John" response simply stated, "Jim, I don't think we should see each other anymore."

Rejection, despair, and intense emotional pain consumed me. The pain and suffering eventually turned into anger about what I let myself do and how Joel had deceived me.

I told Sharon I had to call him and have one more conversation. She could not understand me doing that, but I knew that it would give me closure. I could also call him out on his lies in such a way that he might not hurt someone else like he did me.

In the email correspondence, I pointed out to him that his not going out in public with me, going outside to take and make calls, and driving two different cars to my house were just a few things that exposed his other life to me. "I'm not going to tell your wife as long as you come clean with me and never do this to someone else," I wrote.

Within a few hours, I received his response, "Jim, I appreciate your discretion in this matter. Best of luck to you."

A few months later, I received a phone call from Joel "Jim, buddy, how are you doing? I know I couldn't get together the last time we talked, but I was just wondering if you'd like to take a dip in your hot tub this evening and have some great sex?"

CHAPTER 30

WHEN PASSION RULES

In the late 1990s, increased understanding about the transmission of HIV and AIDS made safe sex more critical. Before the discovery of life-sustaining drugs, men with HIV or AIDS looked sick and, therefore, were identifiable. They were often pale, very skinny, and looked emaciated. Now men could appear healthy and tell you they were negative when they weren't. The playing field seemed to constantly change except that condoms were still man's best friend. I often asked guys to pull out even if they were wearing a condom just to be sure it had not broken.

I decided to bowl in gay bowling tournaments across the country. Traveling with bowling buddies was great fun.

I met a guy online prior to traveling to a bowling tournament happening on July 4th, 2009, in Indianapolis. We decided to spend time together after I arrived. When we met, I noticed he had a small bulging stomach and was thin in general, common side-effects of HIV meds. When I questioned him, he guaranteed me that he was negative, but I trusted condoms more than him and required that he use one.

He was strictly a top when it came to intercourse. We were having a great time and I could tell he was getting close to ejaculation. Suddenly, he pulled out, ripped off the condom and climaxed on me.

"I haven't gotten off yet," I said in frustration, thinking he was timing himself with me.

"I can take care of that," he sneered as he began to re-enter me.

Although it seems there is often time to do the right thing during an assault, sometimes you're caught in the moment and things happen so quickly that it's over before you realize it. Why didn't I just push him away, get up, and save myself? Though I got him out of me quickly, I knew it only took a moment or a small trace of semen to transmit HIV.

"Don't worry," he grunted. "My partner is positive, but like I already told you before, I am negative."

Oh God, he never told you he had a partner and now he says his partner is positive, but he is negative. This is not good.

I knew I faced a dangerous outcome. In a moment of passion, I had allowed another to control my fate.

The next day on the plane back to San Diego, I prayed that I was okay. The lady at the health department advised me to wait before testing to cover the normal four to six-week incubation period.

As I waited for the nurse to return to the room after drawing blood six weeks later, I felt this could end in me being positive. Although chronic sinus problems and allergies had always made me feel like shit, I'd been feeling worse than usual since returning from Indianapolis. The nurse gave me no clue in her facial expression as she entered the room and laid the results page in front of me.

"Mr. Rostello, your test results show you are negative. Congratulations."

I began to cry, thankful for not testing positive. I dug deep in the condom jar sitting on the information table next to the entrance of the clinic and left with a handful of my best friends.

With the scare of my life behind me, I became determined to find out why I felt so bad all the time. I wanted to enjoy all the great things about retirement in San Diego. My mother had suffered from chronic allergies. I remembered as a child that she felt she couldn't be the mother she wanted to be because of her frequent sinus headaches. In the Midwest, allergies can be so bad that you actually feel like you have the flu (often called "hay fever"). Though I'd inherited my mother's problems, I thought San Diego would be better for me. My sinus specialist quickly reminded me that "sinus central" San Diego meant I'd have never-ending allergy issues since nothing that grows there ever dies. To add more bad news, the biggest offender was palm tree pollen. Growing up devoid of that vegetation had probably left me without an immunity to it.

After years of misery, I decided on my last hope: that dreaded sinus surgery. It's a procedure that makes everyone cringe. I chose the week after Labor Day weekend for the surgery and planned a trip to Las Vegas for Labor Day weekend. I prayed that partying and gambling would keep my mind off things.

I barely made it back from Las Vegas. Just three days before my sinus procedure, I felt so miserable with a sinus infection that I dragged myself to the doctor for some antibiotics. The office staff couldn't help because the physician was out of the office, so I crawled into the emergency room not even sure where I had left my car. After the normal wait from hell, the ER doctor immediately admitted me to the hospital with a 105-degree temperature and turned my case over to a specialist. I disclosed my recent negative results from HIV and hepatitis tests. He also noted that the high fever and aggressive onset of my illness were not characteristic of those diseases. When I heard him mention MRSA to another doctor, I knew I could be in big trouble.

After a week of being subjected to every test known to man, my fever remained strong. On a Friday I will never forget; the attending physician doctor entered my room and motioned the nurse to leave. He shut the door and pulled the curtain around my bed, the standard procedure for giving bad news.

"Mr. Rostello, I have news on your condition. You are HIV positive with an acute onset. With all the research going on by the government, you'll be okay and will just need to find a specialist and get on the medication. I will pass this information on to your regular doctor." He was dismissive and almost seemed like he had no sympathy for my HIV status. My first encounter with HIV prejudice sank deep in my mind.

The day of unrelenting shock and fear finally gave way to a subdued sunset through tinted hospital windows with an 'end of the world' shade of light. A nurse entered the room with a sleeping pill around 9:00 p.m. I still remember my emotional pain as the sleep medication took effect.

There is no worse feeling in life than the morning after a traumatic event. The moment you open your eyes, reality slaps you hard making real the knowledge that the event was not just a bad dream. The emotional chill and surreal feelings that I experienced could not be put into words.

The worst physical pain in the world isn't as dangerous or miserable as emotional suffering so deep and overwhelming that shutting out others becomes the only way to cope. Denial, non-acceptance, guilt, and self-hate became my existence.

I found myself telling friends not to visit, and that I needed no help from them. Informing my brother of my diagnosis would just verify my homosexuality and that was not an option. With the fever easing, my doctor sent me home with so many prescriptions I became even more convinced I didn't want to face another day. I spent every minute focused on how the end of my life was imminent.

Who in my life will still care about me and be able to look at me as they have in the past? Who will not think about me being positive every time I sneeze or get close to them for a hug? How will I tell every guy that seems interested in me that I am positive knowing there will be a quick excuse to not go for that cup of coffee? Will I be strong enough to believe that God doesn't hate me? Did he lay this on me because I'm homosexual? Religious friends claimed that very thing.

I didn't sleep for at least a week. As my neighbor helped me home from the hospital, I felt like a different person. Seeing the mementos of my trips or my beautiful paintings no longer brought me happiness. My sleepless nights seemed endless. Every sight and sound seemed like it didn't belong. I didn't want to face another day.

One morning, I stumbled into the hall bathroom to shave and take a long bath. I locked my elbows so that my arms stretched out, supporting my weight on the vanity. The inside of my arms were turned toward the mirror with the palms of my hands gripping the edge of the sink. I stared into the mirror for the first time since my diagnosis.

I saw a person I no longer wanted to be. I quickly turned around to the bathtub and reached into the soap holder for the bar of soap. Turning back to the mirror, holding the edge of the soap, I wrote, "I HATE YOU." Then, I spun around and threw the soap into the tub. It swirled around the perimeter and flew out onto the floor. After sitting on the floor and sobbing, I stumbled back to the bedroom feeling weak due to sleep deprivation.

I fell forward and landed on the bed. I scooted up to rest my weary head on the pillow and gazed at the ceiling in my bedroom. The room began to evaporate around me. I felt myself falling into a half-state of sleep, still cognizant of my surroundings but caught in a state of reverie about a childhood event:

"Jimmie Joe, Jimmie Joe," Mother shouted from my bedroom, summoning me away from the living room floor where I was building houses with my Dad's playing cards. "I bought you a cowboy shirt from a Monkey and Wards sale catalog!"

She held the shirt up for me to see as I charged into the room to reveal its wonderful brown and blue checkered pattern with beige string for the yoke and beautiful pearl buttons.

"I love it, Mom!" I shouted, jumping up and down while ripping off my shirt to try on the new treasure.

"Oh, my goodness," my mother exclaimed as I buttoned up the shirt. "The collar is uneven. It has to go back."

Devastation washed over me. I knew that my days of getting new cowboy shirts were almost over now that I approached 11 years old. This was the best western shirt I'd ever seen. The following Saturday morning as my mother dressed for her weekly trip downtown, I begged to go with her to guard the fate of my new shirt. I came up with excuse after excuse not to be left at home. No reason I gave overcame my mother's emphatic "no."

I tried one last excuse, "Mom, I gotta go today. I need a new fountain pen that has just come out that uses ink cartridges that just snap into the pen. I gotta have it for my penmanship class. I won't have to haul ink to school to keep filling up my old pen. These pens are so cool. Wait till you see them."

I knew my mother was becoming annoyed and her delayed response alerted me that she was not biting on my plea. "You want to go to town and follow me everywhere just for a new pen that you simply must have today? I think there's a snake in the grass here. You've gotta have something else on your mind young man... Well, I guess the new pen is necessary. Okay, you can come along, but you better stay right with me. And no running off to look at toys and stuff. Remember that time two weeks before Christmas when you snuck upstairs at Western Auto to look at toys and I lost you? I found you in the middle of a circle of people during a snowstorm crying like crazy. If you sneak away today, you're in big trouble."

As we approached the mail order catalog desk in the basement of the store, I quickly used my elbows to launch my body up on the counter and locked my dangling feet on the tiny edge of the baseboard to keep myself in the middle of the action.

After verifying the crooked collar, the salesclerk asked, "Irene, do you wanna reorder this shirt?" She began to snap her gum and play with her pin-curled hair using her fingers.

"No, let's just send it back. Jimmy has umpteen cowboy shirts that he soon won't need anymore."

I tugged until I lifted myself even higher on the counter to reach for the shirt. The salesclerk pulled it away to stamp it and throw it into a big box of return items. I never did like this woman, and now she was my foe. She took off her glasses and let them dangle from her neck-chain before letting them rest on her two big mommy things. I hated her mousy blond hair and big bright red lips. "Will that be all today, Irene?"

"Oh please, Mom," I interrupted. "Don't send my shirt back. I'll do anything. I'll clean my room every day. I'll even get a job to pay for it myself."

The cranky salesclerk started to laugh. "And what kind of job do you plan to get, little boy?"

"Why don't you mind your own business," I snapped. "And I hate your cheap smellin' perfume. It stinks!"

Mother quickly backhanded me hard enough to knock my elbow off the counter, and I plummeted to the old, brown, tile floor.

"Why are you sticking up for her, Mom? You always say that you've never liked her."

"Watch your mouth young man," my mom snarled, as she turned red in embarrassment. "I don't think the seamstress can even fix this shirt, and we're short on money this month anyway. You have to learn this is just the way things go sometimes in life and quit being a baby about this. Juanita, just refund the money now please."

"Will that be all, Mrs. Rostello?" The salesclerk asked sarcastically.

Lying on my bed, the ceiling's imperfections became more visible as I returned to consciousness. I wanted to die, to let my disease take away my embarrassment and self-hatred. Suddenly, I remembered what stood out on that big red rubber stamp that the salesclerk used that morning to return the package containing my cowboy shirt. It was what I had now become and would forever be: DAMAGED GOODS.

CHAPTER 31

WHAT HAS HAPPENED?

Within a year of becoming HIV positive, medications had vastly improved my T-cell count and my viral load was nondetectable. Everything looked good on paper, but the inner shame I felt and my new status in the world weighed heavily on my mental well-being. Dating now meant seeing other positive guys, and some only played it unsafe at a time when it was still unknown if there were multiple strains of HIV. Some doctors also believed that if a medication had stopped working for a person, it could cause that drug to lose its effectiveness for their partner if they were also taking that drug.

Dating only positive guys greatly limited my dating opportunities. Joel was still on my mind even though I knew I had done the right thing by respecting his marriage. If he hadn't deceived me, I would have never had sex with the guy that infected me and would have lived happily ever after with Joel.

The HIV drug I was taking gave me horrific nightmares. I would wake up with anxiety and acute depression. One morning, I woke from a dream of my mother walking on my face in a pair of her pointiest high-heeled shoes that I remembered her wearing during my childhood. I became engulfed by anxiety and fear, which kept me from getting out of bed. A panicked feeling left me shaking and grasping for some sort of calmness.

Getting out of bed, showering, and shaving became a challenge. I would stand under the shower nozzle until the hot water turned cold and forced me to reach for a towel. Daily routines were sometimes impossible. On several occasions, I had to leave a shopping cart half-filled with groceries only to drive home in a panic.

My doctor put me on a well-known antidepressant that only caused more anxiety. I spent most days just trying to maintain the house and lying in bed. Sometimes, I would have enough energy to get on male hookup sites or watch TV. When someone would mention meeting, I would say yes and then cancel, knowing I didn't have the energy to get ready.

I noticed several ads on the hookup websites advertising different forms of testosterone, which claimed to increase energy and sex drive, so I asked my doctor if that could be my problem. Tests showed my testosterone level was 40 while a normal level was several hundred. The doctor started with shots and then topical gels. That was my first insight into the importance of managing your own health care.

The testosterone treatments brought my energy back to a level that allowed me to live more normally, but I had to get my depression and anxiety under control. My background in psychology, the influence of Mr. Williamson, and the depiction of depression and its management from "Ordinary People" gave me the insight to see a psychiatrist. I couldn't do this alone, and now the time had come for me to become proactive.

I called my insurance company to get a referral for a psychiatrist, thinking they would have a list of good doctors in the field. I would have to pay a $700 deductible before receiving any mental health benefits. There was no coverage for hypnosis, meditation guidance, or acupuncture. They deemed most Asian therapies as non-scientific. Good ole Anglo-Saxon Christian America!

Arriving at the psychiatrist's office, I walked into a very small waiting room with a sign next to a door that read, "Be seated and ring the doorbell." The doctor finally came out and led me into his office.

"Did you bring the $150 payment that I requested when you made this appointment? I always collect fees before we can begin the session."

"I did, Dr. Fells. But my insurance will pay after I meet my deductible."

"Today's intake appointment will take 40 minutes. Future sessions will be 15 minutes, and I'll collect $100. My accountant will send you records of our sessions, and it's up to you to file with your insurance for compensation. Write your check to Dr. Clayton Fells so we can get started."

Damn, how much can we talk about in just 15 minutes?

"Ok, doctor," I responded.

"Jim, today's session is longer so I can get some medical history from you and the subsequent time frames of fifteen minutes will be used to determine and regulate your anti-depressant medications."

What about my therapy?

"Now, Jim, you are having depression and anxiety? Unusual symptoms found in combination? Can you describe these episodes of anxiety and what seems to precipitate them?

Damn, how do I do that? If I knew what was causing my anxiety and nightmares, I probably wouldn't have them.

"Uh, doctor, I just feel surreal and shaken."

"Have you been more depressed lately? And do you have any history of unusual thoughts or behaviors?"

"Well, I have always been a perfectionist and sometimes a bit obsessive and compulsive."

"Give me an example," the doctor said.

"Just little things, doctor, like being real particular about a good haircut and obsessing over the sheets being exactly even on both sides when I put them on the bed."

"Tell me more about your haircuts."

"Sometimes I redo the haircut when I get home because it's not exactly right. I'll cut it again myself and then again the next day until it's just right. I can spend a long time on that. My barber told me hair lays in different ways all the time and it's never going to be perfect, but that doesn't stop me."

"Oh, I see," the doctor replied. His tone and facial expression indicated that my behavior was linked to my depression.

"Is this causing my problems?" I asked.

"It's all interrelated; however, that is something you'll have to take up with a therapist. Our 15-minute meetings are for medications only. I am going to give you a newer anti-depressant today, and you'll come back to see me in two weeks."

"Doctor, do I see someone else about my obsessive-compulsive behavior or do you help me with that along with my medicine?"

"I don't get involved in therapy or recommend a certain lay therapist. Your insurance should give you references just like they did for psychiatrists. Any more questions? Let's schedule your next visit as time is almost up."

Though beginning to feel very angry, I dutifully got up, took my prescription, and headed out of his office through the sitting area, letting the door close on its own as I hurried off.

"What the fuck just happened? He calls himself a psychiatrist? The Goddam son-of-a-bitch is an imposter and bastardizing psychiatry! You have to be shitting me that this is what the world's coming to. Where in the hell is client-centered therapy? He wouldn't have a job if it weren't for psychotherapy. That no-good prick. He just wants to give me more drugs. That's just what happened in "Ordinary People." When Conrad asked his outpatient psychiatrist if he needed more drugs to feel less like he was on stage, the doctor said he had been on too many anti-depressants at the mental hospital. Sure, Freud might have given cocaine to his patients, but he also used talk therapy. For years people have joked about lying on the couch and exploring their thoughts. Boy, I didn't get a fucking couch today!" I ranted and raved down the elevator and out the building entrance.

As I crossed the street, a driver had to screech to a halt to avoid hitting me. I nodded and gave him a passing hand to move on. Reaching my car, I threw open the car door, tossed my checkbook over to the front passenger seat, and slammed myself down.

I leaned back in the front seat while shouting cuss words. I thought about something my father had said many years ago when a policeman had given him a speeding ticket, "Iffa I wasa driving down the road and saw thatta guy drowning anda there wasa lifesaving things all around, I wouldn'ta throws him one."

I couldn't decide if I felt exactly that way, so I settled for just wishing I had the supernatural power to take away all his present and future patients. Then the disgusting bastard would have to beg for his next meal.

I started the car and realized that out of nowhere, my depression was gone!

I'll be damned. My depression is at least somewhat functionally caused. I can get better and have a better life without all those antidepressants that don't work for me.

I shouted to myself, "See there, you stupid, son-of-a-bitch doctor—you're wrong and letting patients down by not even working with a lay therapist."

But as the weeks passed and my depression deepened, I realized that getting mad had helped me just for a minute when I was leaving the doctor's office. I also realized that seeing a "real" psychiatrist or a behavioral therapist might help me. When I called my insurance for a referral, they recommended a clinic for treating depression. When I called and requested one-on-one counseling, they informed me that most insurance companies only refer group therapy centers. I'd never liked groups and had always preferred being close to just one person.

I finally decided on attending a free therapy group for HIV patients experiencing depression. I thought maybe HIV was still unconsciously affecting me, and it was possible that the members of that group could help me process my feelings. At the first meeting, I learned that each week the group discussed the problems each group member had experienced that week.

One guy started his turn by asking us to help him decide on a different car since his current vehicle had died. He couldn't decide on getting a Smart car or taking a good deal on a used car offered by a relative. This went on for 45 minutes. I wasn't interested in all that bullshit. I wanted to know the personal dynamics of each person's depression. I quit that group after a few weeks and decided to turn to online information. I discovered that my recent angry outbursts could be indicative of suicidal tendencies, information I had hoped to learn in group therapy.

I decided to give psychiatrists one more chance. Right away, my new psychiatrist wanted to put me on Prozac because it was "tried and true." I remembered how it had numbed my students in the classroom and hampered their ability to pay attention. I decided to trust my intuition and not take it. I knew that someday and somehow; I would find a better path for introspection and insight into my troubled existence.

CHAPTER 32

NOT AFRAID TO TELL YOU WHO I AM

A new path in life began the day a bowling buddy and I were driving to our Thursday night league play. He had brought me a brochure and stuck it between the console and the front seat of my car. He mentioned that San Diego Community College offered 1,000 continuing adult education classes. I laughed at the thought of competing with women in a cooking class, "I'd like to show those bitches that I can cook circles around them," I said.

Brian chuckled then said, "Jim, I think you'd like this class on creative writing. It could be a great outlet for you."

This could be a great way to process the things I need to talk about through writing and sharing with people I don't know.

Because my instincts told me that this was a good idea, I decided to attend. Writing had always been one of my passions. After the first session, I felt that the group was friendly, talented, and welcoming to me as a new member. My being a novice creative writer didn't matter to them. They encouraged me to come along and write for the simple joy of writing. The ease I felt allowed me to share the truth about my life, including my sexuality, to a group of almost total strangers. They accepted me.

A close friend had mentioned walking an old, gravel road along a lake near her summer home in Canada and had told me about the wonderful life she'd had with her husband, Tom, the friend of mine who had died within a year of retirement. She remained one of the few close friends always there for me. I decided to write her a poem. When I read the poem in class, a great response came from the group. Their critique encouraged me to share a couple of short essays about my life as a gay boy in the 1960s and '70s. Many group members then pressed me to write memories about my life believing the process could help unravel unresolved issues and feelings.

"You might even consider a personal autobiography," suggested a sweet, wise writer named Mary. "It could help young gay men out in the world understand how things were so different back in those days. It could show them how not to be afraid of who they are."

Each time when I sat down and wrote about feelings or events from my life, I saw how they had affected my entire life and personality. Within a month, writing helped release the emotions that had built up inside me over a lifetime. Feelings gushed from my heart onto the written page. After reading an excerpt in class, I would drive to a parking lot, read my story again, and let myself cry. To my surprise, it became a miraculous therapy.

The writing group emerged as the impetus for a continuous journey of self-discovery. The most important things were the deep, new friendships I'd made. My friends stood beside me, helping me take each step down to the basement of my emotions.

A few conservative Christians gave rough critiques and expressed dismay at my precise personal dialogue. This time, unlike in previous experiences, I knew they were in the minority. They questioned my behavior as a child and as a teacher. Amazingly, their intentions did not hurt or squelch me as they had in the past. I just wrote honestly about my life more and more.

Our skilled and articulate group leader, Olivia, gave us the strategies necessary to become good writers. Her quick editing skills wonderfully balanced an encouragement to write from the soul and successfully get those words down on paper. I would compare her to a nun dressed in street clothes, full of wisdom and knowledge. She embodied compassion and insight. Her greatest gift came to me one day at the end of class. In my reading, I had lashed out at God and the Christian Right for not accepting me. However, she knew that my anger was not the solution to finding peace. As she gathered up her papers, I walked over to Olivia and bent down on one knee next to her.

"Olivia, can you help me?" I asked. "I'm beginning to be okay with where I am, you know, with God. But I feel like everyone thinks I'm not following a path commanded by Him. I don't understand when people say to me that God loves me even though I'm a sinner by being gay."

Olivia turned to me, put her hand on my shoulder, and looked directly into my eyes. "Jim, own your God."

Those four simple words changed my life forever. I began to embrace a spirituality that allowed me to rise above all the noise from religion and the Bible's dictates. I finally had a handle on the most important struggle in my life. Nothing could be more wonderfully spiritual than that simple truth. I began to view the life of Christ as seen through my own heart.

A wonderful writer and friend, Delores, showed me that a religious person can also be spiritual. She accepted my readings with no demands that I accept her thoughts on my gay lifestyle. She just spoke of the love of God and how He cared for all of His children. Though I knew she didn't believe in gay marriage, she avoided that possible wedge in our communication. She knew when to keep her beliefs private, and I came to recognize her deep spirituality. She helped by showing me how to not take my frustrations out on God. Though I'd chosen the path of Native American spiritualism, I began to be at peace with most of the world and with each person's struggle to truly "own" their higher power.

It's ironic that friendships that seem to start slow sometimes grow to be rewarding and solid. One group member, Sherry, directed my struggles to a deeper level. As a novice writer, my weak mechanics strained her patience. In reality, however, like the others in the group, she simply wanted me to be the best writer I could be. One day at the end of her critique, she wrote, "Keep digging, Jim."

Damn. I'm going as deep as I can. What the hell does she want from me? I left the class that day, drove to my secluded spot, and reread my writing. An amazing and new revelation about my personal history gushed to the surface, along with my tears. I really did have to go deeper to get out all my past struggles.

One day I read a particularly wrenching chapter about my homosexuality and the Catholic ritual of confession. Sherry, who was also Catholic, turned to me and said, "Let it go, Jim. I have let things about our church rest, and you must do the same. It's the key to finding happiness." She helped me bring things to the conscious level. With her encouragement, my writing did go deeper. Sherry did not let me slide by on surface pity.

I grew to love other class members including Lidia, Doria, and Will, who all became very empathic friends and pillars in my life. They showed me love, respect, and admiration. By recognizing that my story needed to be told, they motivated me to share it with the world.

Anna Bess probably influenced the writing of my memoirs more than anyone else. She recognized the sensitivity and honesty it took to share my life with the group.

One day, she said to me, "Your bravery and one-of-a-kind openness need to be shared. I am here for you and will do anything I can to get your memoirs published."

I actually read this chapter at a gathering because I thought at the time that it was the ending of my memoirs. Many of my fellow writers showed up to be there for me.

I began pretending to be a therapist and started a long process of self-analysis.

• • •

Jim, you know that your behavior had become way too promiscuous in retirement and that you were probably getting too careless. You should be thankful that you didn't get sick back in the 80s when it was a death sentence. Look at all your friends that are gone. *You don't want to look back five years from now and realize all the energy that you wasted on something you can't change.*

• • •

For God's sake, Jim, everything happens for a reason when you trust destiny. Maybe the sinus surgery would have gone badly or a worse thing was on the horizon; you must accept this phase of your life and know that anyone can make a mistake. Everyday people get into their cars in a hurry and drive a bit too fast and end up paralyzed or dead. So, you didn't react quick enough to the guy re-penetrating you. You can forgive yourself for that, can't you? Wow, Jim, that's what the psychotherapist said to Conrad in "Ordinary People!"

• • •

All my life, I believed the adage "to err is human, to forgive divine." I have been working to completely forgive the person who gave me HIV. I finally realized that forgiveness means not only forgiving other people but also forgiving yourself. We all make mistakes.

Another gift from the writing class came one day over our midmorning break. After reading a wrenching chapter from my book, I asked a few members, "If my work ever gets published, will anyone really want to read it?"

An especially astute member of the group looked at me and asked, "Jim, who is your real audience? Who is this for? You need to think about that."

I felt like someone had slapped me on the back of the head. Throughout the class, that question kept leaping into my mind. Was my writing to please everyone or impact those who had a different agenda? I had realized the most important audience was my family: my deceased mother, father, brother, and me.

One afternoon, I was re-reading some of my memoirs and realized that I needed to go to a special place that was spiritual for me. I hurried to the parking lot and broke the speed limit driving to my favorite spot at the tip of Point Loma where the rocky coastline meets the crashing surf. The ocean had always been my friend in life. My feelings surged then raged inside me. I slammed on the parking brake, jumped out of the car, and ran to the top of a bluff. A path wound its way down to the rugged shore. I began to charge down the gullied cliff. A terrifying sound stopped me dead in my tracks—the chitt, chitt, chitt of a Pacific Rattlesnake. It lay coiled in the center of the trail. Normally, I would have screamed and run the opposite direction. As a kid, I would jump and run into another room when a rattlesnake appeared on TV or hide under seats in movie theaters.

But not that day. I grabbed several large rocks and bombarded the snake until it slithered under the scrub brush away from the path. I dashed down to the water's edge, almost tripping into the ocean to stand on the sunbathed rocks where the endless pounding surf greeted land.

The perfect blue sky cast its magical spell that creates the stunning trademark Pacific blueness. I gazed out to where the blazing horizon met the sea. I felt like I was part of an old Cinemascope movie. Cameras looked down from the sky and caught me revolving in a complete circle of land and sea. For the first time, I found myself engulfed in a bigger picture.

The sea opened its depths, asking me to trust it as a friend. The sea can give all or take it all away. It is neither owned nor controlled. Its gifts are given only when we open our hearts and minds to experience its endless sights and sounds.

The frothy waves, ocean mist, and warming sun began to speak to me, "Yes, Jim, your family was dysfunctional. Your father's Italian temper and authoritarian ways hurt you. But, in his own way, he made you the sensitive person you are today." I breathed in the sea breeze as it whispered, "Your father loved you."

I began to think about my brother as he lay dying from cancer. He had assured my sister-in-law that I would make the trip all the way to Chicago to see him one last time. When I arrived at his bedside, I attempted to hug him. He winced and begged me not to grab his hand too tight. His once athletic body had surrendered to weakness and pain.

"Thank you for coming, Jim," he said. Some silence passed as we both found comfort in staring at the flickering TV. Finally, my brother began to speak as he looked away from me.

"I need to tell you what I overheard Dad asking Mom one day. He said, 'Do you think Jimmy loved me and knows how proud I am of him? He's so smart; the intelligence of this family. He's a good little guy. I know he's ashamed of me being Italian and that I couldn't be what he needed. I don't think the extra quarters I gave him from my pocket when he was a little boy did the trick. Guess he'll never know how much I love him.'"

I stood closer to my brother as he motioned for me to give him water. He looked directly into my eyes and began to frown as he spoke. "I promised Mom that I'd take care of you, and now it's too late for that. She always told me you were her baby boy and that I must look out for you because you carried a burden that no one else will ever know. She loved you."

The next day, I left my brother and returned to San Diego. When I walked through the kitchen, I found the message on my phone, my sister-in-law letting me know he was gone. Everyone agreed he died a happy man. Though my brother had been hot-tempered and cranky, he was giving and extroverted with others, and a good, loyal brother. They say you never really know a family member until you have to share an inheritance. Several years earlier, about a year after my mother had died, I received a final check from my brother for $220 to settle the exact amount of my share of the inheritance. He also did not take executor fees.

Sitting by the ocean, I watched the deep orange afternoon sun cast a spell on the blue ocean. I felt exhausted and rested on a huge black boulder. As I gathered my thoughts, memories of the morning after my father died captured my mind. He had passed in his sleep; no pain, no suffering. The morning after my father died, I came into the kitchen to find my mother staring out the window above the kitchen sink toward the backyard barbecue pit. Every evening in spring, summer, and fall, he sat outside with his lawn chair tipped on its back legs, his feet resting on the edge of the pit. He would hold a frosty 16-ounce can of Schlitz in one hand. In the other hand, he held a favorite KOOL cigarette just above the filter and between his middle fingers. Clouds of smoke drifted from his nose into the air when he exhaled.

"The house seems so empty, Jim," Mom reminisced in a soft tone. "You know, it's a funny thing son. Last night your father left our bed to sleep on the cooler back porch to escape the heat. Earlier, while he was getting ready to fry fish for supper, he told me something I'll never forget. He said he had forgiven everyone that had done him wrong in life. All the strained friendships and relationships, all the disappointments. He blamed no one for anything. He was just ready to let things be and whatever happens on this earth doesn't matter anymore."

Mom began to weep. I went to her and held her in my arms.

On the beach that day, my own disappointments drifted out with the tide. Now I loved my parents for doing the best they could under many different circumstances. You can't expect anyone to do more than they are able to.

The day of my ocean experience, my epiphany led me to take responsibility for helping my depression and disappointments in life. Understanding that my parents were bound by their own issues and struggles allowed me to reach out and forgive them.

As much as I'd never liked the Midwest, there were things about life there that were positive, realistic and tried and true, like the way that people said "honey" or "sweetheart" and handshakes cuffed within the loose hand are treasures in life. Today's world now looks at terms of endearment as sexual harassment.

There were also so many home remedies, like gargling with salt water for tooth problems that worked better than all of the high-priced drugs.

Thinking back to my early years, I even remember self-therapies that helped with the mind and soul. One thing my mother did for me was to encourage me to sit down and write a letter to the difficult situations. She said, "Even if you don't mail it, it will help you."

Writing always puts things into a good place. So, I decided to write a letter to my deceased mother to set things straight between us. My journey to inner peace had begun after accepting myself.

I am not afraid to tell myself who I am.

Dear Mom,

You will always be in my spiritual world and the soul of who I am. I have come to respect and understand you.

Those days filled with singing, shopping, movies, filled with so much energy and attention, are treasured memories. Then, there were the times you would retreat to your bedroom, or send me out to play by myself.

Like you, I have extreme allergies that left you exhausted and sick. Mentally, I share the same ups and downs now called bipolar disorders. The drug treatments of today have not worked for me.

Although I will never forget the night you and dad sent me away when Linda broke our engagement. Now, I can focus on the good.

I try to be a different person and never send someone away unexplained. I try to reach out with honest talk and disclosure. When a relationship must end, I strive for us both to be ok. A hug, a kiss, a good-bye always.

I love you Mom,

Jim

CHAPTER 33

A NEW HEART

Writing my memoirs in a critique group environment motivated me to process difficult memories. Putting the past in the past took me to ground zero and the acceptance to move on with the future. I now realized that a better life meant implementing changes to the present and future. Living in the past would mean a miserable unfulfilled life. My background in psychology and writing had also showed me that no one knows me better than me or can help me more than me.

I knew that it was time for a change by moving to Palm Springs, a destination for retired gays. There were many older HIV-positive guys there who I wouldn't find in San Diego. My current home in San Diego was an older house in a family neighborhood which limited my lifestyle. I also hoped my allergies might improve.

I now had the determination to make the move to Palm Springs in 2012 at age 63. Buying a house and moving by myself at my age was not easy. Having depression and feeling physically bad made the process challenging. I succeeded in getting my San Diego house on the market and sold and bought a house in Palm Springs and completed an entire renovation. The contractor was amazed by how my redesign had transformed the house. Some mornings on busy days, I would lay in bed and think I would never make it through the day.

In Palm Springs, practically everyone you come into contact with is gay. Even conservative straight people did not consider the gay lifestyle in their political and religious opinions. Retired movie stars and artists also created a wonderful, unique city. Mid-century architecture and modernism even began to grow on me. I began meeting a lot of retired positive guys and would find the energy for limited friendship and sexual companionship.

I met a special person named Justin, who was retired from the corporate world in San Francisco. We would finish each other's sentences and thoughts. We were dating at the time I decided to complete the second phase of my plan for a full and better life: a condo in San Diego. The summer heat in the desert cannot be described. It is brutal.

I finally learned that changing goals for love is not always best and low self-esteem can sabotage life. Justin and I needed to grow together without expectations. Besides that, San Diego could always become a second place for both of us. Justin also had expressed his concern for a successful relationship given his nature. He was so cautious not to lead me on. For months, he would say, "You are important to me." One day he finally said, "I love you." With that, he gave me all he could give.

Back in San Diego, I stumbled onto a very aggressive and shrewd real estate agent who found me a one-of-a-kind condo as the winter holidays approached. Her negotiating skills and ability to attain the best deal astounded me.

Around Christmas, I grabbed up a perfect residence in the most respected condo building in downtown San Diego with a cash offer. The views of the bay from the balcony were outstanding.

I could watch the sailboats and see Point Loma from the great room and the master bedroom. The time of year and owners' wealth led them to take my offer. I pulled off an update and move of the necessary furniture with the help of my handyman. It did help me gain a little more control of my issues. Going back and forth between my two places also kept me going emotionally.

One night at my condo in San Diego, I woke up from a dream about pain. When I grabbed the headboard of my bed as

I woke, the pain was real. I sat on the side of my bed wondering if I could drive to the emergency room because I didn't want to bother anyone. One of my major quirks in life is a distaste of having to call 911. That would bring flashing lights and sirens, which would draw attention to me, especially in the middle of the night. After taking a couple of TUMS for my raging, upset stomach, I threw on clothes and headed down to the front desk.

When he saw me, the lobby manager walked over and tried to get me to sit down. "You look bad, Mr. Rostello. I'm calling the paramedics." I started to hobble to the parking lot elevator to just go it alone rather than have a valet bring my car up. The manager finally agreed to walk ahead of my car and guide me out of the narrow lanes of the underground parking structure.

After maneuvering through the narrow ramps in pain, I finally pulled out of the garage and onto Market Street. I felt like a cement block occupied my entire left side. Too preoccupied with telling myself I could make it to the emergency room, I missed the hospital exit on the freeway. Somehow, I made it to the next exit and turned around. Once parked, I hobbled into the emergency room, holding my left arm. The savvy night nurse rushed me to a treatment room without doing any paperwork—I looked that bad. After being stabilized, a catheterization revealed that I had total heart artery blockage. The surgeon whispered to the attendant that he couldn't believe I was alive. The dreaded quadruple bypass wouldn't be enough. I needed the quintuple procedure.

The following day, the surgeon said the surgery would be in a couple of days after the Plavix wore off and I was completely stabilized. With the pain now under control, I pleaded with the doctor that I just wanted to go back to my condo to sit on the balcony to watch the sailboats chase each other and die. I was not hip on living, given the pain of the surgery and the recovery that would follow on top of dealing with my depression and nightly anxiety attacks from nightmares.

The surgeon sternly urged me to do the surgery. "Mr. Rostello, you're only 66 years old. Your prognosis is good. Let me do this surgery, and you might feel better than you have in years." His positive attitude and my desire to finally trust someone that wanted to help me brought me around.

"Okay, Doc. I'll have this surgery one time and one time only."

My surgeon was young, confident, and boyishly cute. His bright blue eyes beamed as he walked into my room to find I'd been sitting up for over an hour just 17 hours after a successful surgery. He laughed and bragged, "You look better than I do! You have a new heart, and you're good to go for 15 to 20 years as long as you exercise and watch your diet."

How do I tell this nice, dedicated doctor that I'm not all that excited about living? I'll always be alone and unhappy in the end.

"Does this mean no staying up all night, no drinking, no wild women, and no In-N-Out Burger?" I joked. I wanted to be positive and thankful to my wonderful doctor and not dampen his success with my negative views on life.

"Well, I don't know I would want you to give up all of those things," the surgeon said with a smile. "How about just using a little moderation?"

The next few days after such a difficult bypass remain a blur. Trying to cough up phlegm while clutching a pillow brought seething pain. Pulling the drainage tubes out of my stomach felt like I was losing my insides. Thankfully, we don't relive pain via conscious memories. A couple of days after the surgery, I had enough strength to hold the phone and call my neighbor. She agreed to call Justin and let him know about my surgery.

Immediately, I received the most outstanding flowers from Justin with the lyrics from "Jimmy Mac" on the accompanying card. A couple of young nurses sang the song to me. Each day, Justin would call and ask how I was doing and when I'd be able to go home. He seemed so loving on the phone.

After five days, I knew I might be going home. One day, the head nurse said I would go home the next day and then changed her mind due to my pain level and elevated heartbeat, which was common after having bypass surgery. On day seven, Justin called to see if I was going to be released. Frustrated, I let him know that I didn't know when I'd go home, though it might be later that day if the nurse didn't change her mind.

"Justin, I don't know what's going on. One of my former neighbors from here in San Diego who's my medical advisor offered to take me to the convalescent home as long as it's today since they leave on a big trip tomorrow. I'll be going to a nursing home for about a week since I can't take care of myself. I'll call you when I'm settled at the convalescent home with the phone number there so you can reach me if you want."

In a very memorable moment, Justin announced, "Oh, Jimmy, baby. I'm coming to take care of you. You're going home and I'll be there every minute doing everything for you. I love you. I'll bathe my dog, throw things in the car, and be there in three hours."

He came despite the fact that I didn't want him to see me in my sickly state. I believed that he would lose any sexual interest in me and not love me anymore after seeing me pale and weak with a shriveled-up penis. On my sterile highway to happiness, I had come to believe that sex is love and love means sex. Now, up ahead I'd encounter a right turn onto a beautiful country road guiding me home, to the person I used to be.

Struggling to sit up as the visiting nurse took my blood pressure one day, I said to Justin, "You're not going to want me after seeing me like this."

"Are you kidding?" Justin giggled. "Hell, baby, I find you sexier than ever. I'm going to ravish you as soon as you're better." Though my chest hurt like hell, I cried in joy because I'd found true love.

Justin changed my outlook on everything during this time. He helped me out of bed, stayed by my side every moment, cooked for me, and changed my bedsheets every day. He clapped as I successfully walked to each end of the exterior hallway. We talked about the future and shared an unspoken bond.

During my hospital stay, the nurses and supporting therapists showed me love. After being moved to a regular room, ICU nurses came to visit me there because I was their favorite patient. One nursing aide brought her entire family to see me on their way to church and to give me a rosary. Another caregiver learned the song "The Rose" by Bette Midler and sang it at my bedside. The son of a former coworker in Kansas City, Jeremy, sent me an array of roses and offered to clear his business schedule to fly down from San Francisco if I needed help. I had been one of his favorite teachers. Jeremy had been the student council president and incredibly respected by everyone. He'd become a highly successful corporate VIP. His priority on helping me opened my eyes to the good in the world.

When I returned home to my condo, the desk manager commented that the desk man on duty had called the property manager at 3 a.m. when I left for the emergency room. She called at dawn checking to see if I came back or if anything was heard regarding my whereabouts.

Friends from all aspects of my life called me regularly. When I finally returned to my writing group, one of the most respected and beautiful writers in the group came up during break to welcome me back. She changed my soul when she said, "Jim, I can tell you're a good and nice person. I can see it with your encouragement each time you critique someone and in your actions." I just stood there in humble appreciation.

My surgeon was right. I had a new heart.

CHAPTER 34

I JUST DIDN'T SEE IT

Justin came through in my time of needing home care when I returned home after my heart surgery. His willingness to drive from Palm Springs to San Diego to be there for me boosted my recovery. I needed a person to want me to live for me to want to live. He left a day early as I was able to secure a paid caregiver. He wanted to get home.

Justin and I talked every day, and he came to San Diego several times. I was able to cook a wonderful Thanksgiving dinner. Justin would say, "Nothing makes me hornier than a man that cooks for me." Even with those words, I knew we would never be together. We were too much alike, too old and set in our ways, and hurt too much by others. Every time Justin came to visit, he would get restless after a day or two. He would go in spurts of telling me he loved me and then back off at times. I learned in life not to ask a person for more than they can give whether it be in love, friendship, or life.

When things would not be good, he would draw back in terms of our future. I understood that and felt the same.

I just didn't need to hear it. One day he said, "Jim, I am not in love with anyone; I only love my dog."

I already knew that and didn't need to hear it. We'd discussed not being a couple many times because his dog was his life. I retorted, "Dogs are not humans, and I am not in competition for your love with your dog. Human love and dog love doesn't mean a choice. I'm having trouble understanding why you needed to say that. Maybe we need some time to rethink our friendship."

"Are you breaking up with me? I have to go now," Justin snapped as he hung up the phone.

Several months passed, and I needed to get something I left at his house. He offered to meet me at Starbuck's.

As I approached the coffee shop, I looked inside as a customer was leaving. Justin was moving from one table to another and then to another by a window. He rearranged the condiments and sat down. This will always remain one of my best memories. Sometimes giving relationships space can put everything in perspective. My love for him became forever and unconditional. As we started doing things together again both of us never felt the need to put distance between us. But that's not life's reality sometimes.

Life sucks when the not-so-bad chips away at the all-that-is-so-good. Expectations, unnecessary demands, and perceptions are the great protagonists in failed relationships. Justin's shutdowns during misunderstandings were his unique responses to want to be what I needed, but unable to do so. My long list of desires was nothing compared to what he was trying to be for me. He needed a bypass to rejections he had already endured from important people in his life.

In the end, I knew that freedom from my relationship with him is not what I wanted. My mother always said it takes two to get along and two to part. My long path to the cures I have achieved included Justin, my dog, therapy, and my experiences and introspection from these memoirs. Could I actually love myself just a little bit?

Life's continuum and events built love and kept Justin and me from walking away in tough times. Just a short time before this book was published, Justin said all I needed to hear in a letter:

The Year of the Pandemic

Jim,

I will always love you.

Justin

There had been a lot of "sures" and "unsures" in our process of mutual acceptance of what each of us needed and wanted. Our love has been too limited in dimension and the superlative nature of a real love for us to suffice.

Justin loved the vine-ripened tomatoes I grew for him; I loved giving them to him. I just wished he would help me plant them.

As time passed after my heart surgery, friends would often say that I seemed better as they wanted to encourage me. I didn't recognize my emotional improvement until I was able to take a big step in my life. I was sick and plagued by anxiety every day. I didn't know that I was somewhat better until taking one big step: getting a dog. I always failed with people but could give all of me to a devoted canine friend. I was scared to death that I couldn't do it, but knew I had to try.

I chose a breeder off the internet by chance. She offered mixed breed puppies of a King Charles Cavalier spaniel and poodle. Our spaniels Brownie and Picca had always given me love. My mother always had a poodle as our inside dog. The breeder lived in the rural town of Vista. When I arrived to see the pups, I was told the smaller one with fawn-colored ears and rich, cream color body was sold. She seemed abrupt when she did not allow me to touch any of her puppies. "If you come back, then you can hold the puppy you want."

We talked again on the phone, and I honestly disclosed my depression and how this was a scary challenge for me. I expressed paranoid concerns about caring for a 10-week-old puppy and going through potty training. I assured her that my love of dogs and my past dog were the best days in my life.

"Josephine, I need help," I pleaded. "I know a dog will help me more than a therapist or medicine."

"Jim, come back and see me. I've sold this wonderful mixed breed to many people needing emotional support. I'm swamped, but I'll help you."

I knew she had two litters of puppies, 20 horses, and a mentally challenged 30-year-old son that she had raised alone. Returning to her farm, the dog I liked had not been picked up by the Arizona buyer. She said he was the pick of the litter, and I could have him. I will never forget the feeling when she set him on my lap, and he looked up at me.

She offered to keep the puppy two additional months and potty train him to sleep through the night. All of this for just a few dollars a day. In December, a typical California wildfire forced her to evacuate in just a few hours with the help of the sheriff and fire department. She was strong and saw it through with the fire coming within 300 feet of her house.

The day I brought my dog home, it was cold, and the puppy became car sick and hurled all over the back seat through the window of his crate. He was scared and cried and shivered from the bath I gave him. *What have I done? I can't do this. I can hardly take care of myself. This is not fair to him or me.*

I called Justin and asked him if he would go with me to the local shelter in the morning to find "Paisano" a good home.

"Ah, Jim. I can't tomorrow. I know this dog is right for you. Just keep him for another day and I will bring you a check for whatever you paid for him and you will know he is getting a good home."

I knew he was tricking me to give the dog one more day to win my heart, but that didn't matter. My soul wanted to play along. Two people had stepped in to save my life, and they did.

Today, at night, my dog turns circles as he descends to hit my body in bed to sleep beside me. He watches me and speaks comfort with his eyes when I awake from a bad dream. He is stunningly handsome and doesn't know a stranger. He gets me out of bed and away from anxiety to "go out" and be fed. I love my dog more than anyone or anything in my life.

A few months before my 50-year class reunion in 2017, I received an unexpected phone call from one of my high school classmates from my junior and senior years when I finished high school in the public school system. Gary had been one of those "in crowd" guys that seemed only interested in being cute and could snub an unpopular nerd. His bright blond hair and distinctive dress code made him seem unapproachable.

"Is this Jim Rostello from Moberly, Missouri?" he asked.

"This is he," I acknowledged in hesitation.

"This is Gary Smithson. We had several classes together and always wondered how you ended up getting out of Moberly. Everyone always said you would. Remember when we sat across the aisle from each other in Mr. Harley's English Lit class and I opened up an umbrella while he was lecturing by reading notes on his desk?"

"Of course, who could forget that," I remarked. "How's things back in Moberly?"

"Oh, things never change here except most of the railroad operations are gone and the town and the people are just like they always were. Most of the once big downtown has been torn down and the remaining old grand stores are now thrift and antique shops. Walmart has pretty much raped the city. Are you coming back for our 50th reunion? You haven't made it back once in all these years."

"I pretty much have put those days behind me," I said, establishing my lack of interest.

"Jim, lots of us thought you were a hilarious guy and always seemed to get ahead in class."

"Well, thanks for the compliment, but I never felt other students felt that way. I made it to California and out of Missouri."

"Why would you say that? People thought you were a good guy and would go places. You were known as the only one to get an A in Mrs. Munninger's Comp and Rhet class. She even called you Jimmie."

"What are you talking about?" I questioned.

"Well, surely you know that Rich, your classmate from St. Pius knew that Sister Anna Mary thought the world of you. Rich told Beth Warren that his mom had heard that Sister Anna Mary told Mrs. Munninger to take care of you. She pointed you out in front of church after services. By the way, Rich is still one of the richest guys in town and drinks more than ever. He finally did marry Susie Allen. They are divorced now. She doesn't look like her yearbook picture anymore, that's for sure."

A surreal realization that my treasured Sister Anna Mary had done that for me took me away from the phone conversation for a few seconds. I had lost so many debates and was a terrible actor, but she always took me along to other towns for competitions. She gave me the World History award.

I needed to get off the phone and think about how she did care for me and helped me come out of my shell. "Well, Gary, I am surprised to hear from you and thanks for the call. The only person I would come back to Moberly to see from our high school days would be Cynthia Babbs and she was a year ahead of us. She won homecoming queen and won about every contest. She was sincerely nice to everyone as well as gorgeous."

"Yeah, she went on to a big expensive acting college, but I haven't heard much about her lately. Anyway, Jim, keep in touch and call me sometime. Guess you've made it big in California but it's still nice talking with you. A couple of months ago, I called Darren Bailey that I hung around with. As he hung up after a bunch of yeses and noes to our good times in school, I heard him say, 'Why is he calling me? What a waste of my time.' Darren didn't care about me and I know that you wouldn't have done that to me. Jim, if you decide to come back for the reunion, Nancy, our senior class secretary, has all the details."

"I'll give it some thought," I responded. That ended one of the most important phone calls in my life. Shock and amazement swept over me. I began to question all those years in Moberly.

There was one more thing I had to do for my peace of mind. I had become a successful man and proud of my financial success. With no relatives, I needed to know that my money was distributed in meaningful ways. I set up an art scholarship and a psychology award program at my Alma Mater. Each piece of my art was a memory of a place I had traveled and made some great friends. I learned you don't have to have a long encounter for a friendship to be fulfilling. Friends I never see or know anymore are still part of who I am.

I set up programs for youth bowling given it had been very rewarding since I was 10 years old. I endowed psych scholarships and guest speaking programs for educating therapists in client-centered therapy in honor of Mr. Williamson.

One day, I answered the phone, and it was a call from Mr. Williamson. He had called to thank me for my endowment in his name. We had a long memorabilia-filled chat.

I was finally able to disclose my feelings about my years in Moberly, "Mr. Williamson, you saved my life. I was a nobody and such a loser. I couldn't believe it when you took me and a popular athlete to Truman State to meet our future professor. You made me feel important when my life was a nothing."

"Jim, you were as important then as you are now, you just didn't see it."

ACKNOWLEDGEMENTS

Grateful acknowledgement to Mary F. Platter-Rieger. Mary is a special and true friend who has been instrumental to my success in writing and living. She spent countless hours helping me edit and produce copies to take to my writing seminar. She took photographs and was there anytime I needed her. My memoirs came to life sitting next to Mary at her computer. She has a great husband and 2 wonderful daughters who are my caretakers in living.

Thank you to Ryan Forsythe for book design and publishing assistance.

Finally, very special thanks to Dawn Wilson and Gary Kendall.

ABOUT THE AUTHOR

Sharing from his vegetable and rose garden
Knowing his students remember him
Remembering his uncharted world travel of bygone days
In the play, not the audience
Building and designing homes
Giving accolades and supporting psychology in our lives
DOG-LOVE   DOG-THERAPY   DOG-RESCUE

ABOUT THE COVER DOGS

Paisano, the star of the front cover, is the heart and soul of Jim's sunset days of existence. Paisano will not eat until he is given a nod and cries instead of barks when someone comes to the door thinking he will be petted and loved. He is the most beautiful and best dog in the world.

Luna, on the back cover, is a cousin to Paisano. She has a very special purpose in the lives of the students of San Diego State University. During the pandemic, her first year of life centered on "virtual" therapy. Each day she sits up to the computer to look and listen to a student in need. She never fails to bring joy and peace. Her triumphs of therapy have been praised by those who have experienced her presence. Her trainer notes she's the most intelligent in training history. When school on campus resumes, Luna will do her magic in person. She is part of the Jim Rostello Dog Therapy Endowment. Jim hopes to build a template for school therapy programs.

Made in the USA
Monee, IL
17 June 2023